THE BEDFORD SERIES IN HISTORY AND CULTURE

1989: Democratic Revolutions at the Cold War's End

A Brief History with Documents

Padraic Kenney

Indiana University

Brian Thorp

BEDFORD/ST. MARTIN'S   Boston ♦ New York

For Bedford/St. Martin's

Publisher for History: Mary V. Dougherty
Director of Development for History: Jane Knetzger
Senior Editor: Heidi L. Hood
Developmental Editor: Sylvia Mallory
Editorial Assistant: Jennifer Jovin
Production Supervisor: Andrew Ensor
Executive Marketing Manager: Jenna Bookin Barry
Project Management: Books By Design, Inc.
Index: Books By Design, Inc.
Text Design: Claire Seng-Niemoeller
Cover Design: Richard DiTomassi
Cover Photo: Student Demonstration at Tiananmen Square. Thousands of students
   stage demonstrations in Beijing's Tiananmen Square to protest the Chinese
   government's hardline policies against democratic reform and freedom of speech.
   © Baldev/Corbis.
Composition: TexTech International
Printing and Binding: RR Donnelley & Sons Company

President: Joan E. Feinberg
Editorial Director: Denise B. Wydra
Director of Marketing: Karen R. Soeltz
Director of Editing, Design, and Production: Marcia Cohen
Assistant Director of Editing, Design, and Production: Elise S. Kaiser
Manager, Publishing Services: Emily Berleth

Library of Congress Control Number: 2009928540

Manufactured in the United States of America.

4   3   2   1   0   9
f   e   d   c   b   a

For information, write: Bedford/St. Martin's, 75 Arlington Street,
Boston, MA 02116   (617-399-4000)

ISBN-10: 0-312-48766-5
ISBN-13: 978-0-312-48766-9

Acknowledgments

Acknowledgments and copyrights are continued at the back of the book on pages
187–88, which constitute an extension of the copyright page.

Distributed outside the United States by Palgrave Macmillan.

Foreword

The Bedford Series in History and Culture is designed so that readers can study the past as historians do.

The historian's first task is finding the evidence. Documents, letters, memoirs, interviews, pictures, movies, novels, or poems can provide facts and clues. Then the historian questions and compares the sources. There is more to do than in a courtroom, for hearsay evidence is welcome, and the historian is usually looking for answers beyond act and motive. Different views of an event may be as important as a single verdict. How a story is told may yield as much information as what it says.

Along the way the historian seeks help from other historians and perhaps from specialists in other disciplines. Finally, it is time to write, to decide on an interpretation and how to arrange the evidence for readers.

Each book in this series contains an important historical document or group of documents, each document a witness from the past and open to interpretation in different ways. The documents are combined with some element of historical narrative—an introduction or a biographical essay, for example—that provides students with an analysis of the primary source material and important background information about the world in which it was produced.

Each book in the series focuses on a specific topic within a specific historical period. Each provides a basis for lively thought and discussion about several aspects of the topic and the historian's role. Each is short enough (and inexpensive enough) to be a reasonable one-week assignment in a college course. Whether as classroom or personal reading, each book in the series provides firsthand experience of the challenge—and fun—of discovering, recreating, and interpreting the past.

Lynn Hunt
David W. Blight
Bonnie G. Smith
Natalie Zemon Davis
Ernest R. May

Preface

Images of the fall of communism and of struggles against dictatorship at the end of the twentieth century have become icons of democratic change. They include the jubilant crowds filling the streets of Prague and Berlin; one-time political prisoners embracing their former captors or even addressing their fellow citizens as political leaders; and a lone man standing up to a line of tanks in Beijing. All these images come from 1989, a year that has become emblematic of the popular desire for democracy. Although 1989, during which the Communists yielded control of Eastern Europe, is barely twenty years ago, it belongs firmly to history. And that history remains urgently important to anyone concerned with the future of human rights and democracy.

1989: Democratic Revolutions at the Cold War's End seeks to bring into focus the global transformations that marked the end of the cold war order and shaped the era in which we live. Through six case studies of revolutionary movements (in Poland, the Philippines, Chile, South Africa, Ukraine, and China) from the 1980s and early 1990s—as well as a survey of key ideas about democracy, nonviolence, responsibility, and revolution—this volume explores the common traits of political change on four continents, while also highlighting the different perspectives and different strategies of the people who sought to free themselves from dictatorships.

The stories and ideas in this book evoke the raucous spirit of that age of democratic transformation (which did not begin, or end, in 1989 itself), when the serious work of toppling dictatorships was often suffused with a carnivalesque atmosphere. The volume introduction in Part One examines key trends in the decades leading up to the changes of the late 1980s, tracing the paths that dictatorships and oppositions alike took toward their fateful confrontations. Part Two then takes the reader into the documents that reveal the ideas and movements behind democratic change on four continents. In many ways, this revolutionary era was different from those of the past, which were both more violent and more ideological; only by encountering the actual words and actions of the leaders and the social movements can one understand just how new these revolutions were.

Chapter 1 of Part Two showcases political thinkers from the post–cold war era ranging from Aung San Suu Kyi to Václav Havel, revealing surprising commonalities and deep divergences in ideas about democracy, nonviolence, and political change. The case studies in Chapters 2 through 7 were chosen to reflect the diversity and the interconnectedness of this revolutionary era. The first case study is that of Poland, whose Solidarity movement proved an inspiration throughout the world from its emergence in 1980. Next come the Philippines—where the phrase "people power" entered the modern political lexicon—then Chile, South Africa, Ukraine (during the Soviet Union's breakup in 1991), and China, the one failed revolution. Each chapter begins with an introduction that presents the country and highlights the problems specific to that dictatorship and the challenges that opposition movements faced. Pre-reading focus questions at the end of each chapter's introduction encourage students to consider connections among the cases.

Each of the six case studies features four or more documents representing the visionaries and strategists who sought to catalyze resistance to dictatorships, and the social movements—ranging from street theater to hunger-striking students—that mobilized discontent. These rich primary sources—including posters, meeting transcripts, letters, and eyewitness accounts—have been carefully chosen to capture major themes of each democratic movement and to give students the opportunity to see how ideas are transformed into action. They also allow students to consider how similar goals can be achieved in quite different ways and to ponder why movements for change sometimes fail. A number of these documents have never appeared in English before; others have been collected from private archives and rare publications. A headnote preceding each document offers further context, introducing the author or setting the scene, while gloss notes at the bottom of the pages explain unfamiliar references within the documents.

At the end of the book, a chronology juxtaposes the revolutions of the late cold war and provides the larger context for each revolution at a glance. A set of questions invites closer examination of the documents and suggests avenues for deeper comparative work. Finally, a selected bibliography of secondary works opens up pathways for exploring this revolutionary era.

ACKNOWLEDGMENTS

This book would not have been possible without the assistance of Deanna Wooley, who collected many of the documents and secondary sources. José Najar translated documents from Spanish, and Ramajana Hidić-Demirović provided additional editorial assistance. Teresa Valdés and Lesley Hart kindly located and sent hard-to-find documents. My colleagues at Indiana University provided valuable feedback, as did participants in a conference at Stanford University's European Center; at the Wits Institute for Social and Economic Research, Johannesburg; and at the Centre for African Studies at the University of Cape Town.

I would like to thank the following readers of this manuscript for their many valuable suggestions: Andrew F. Clark, University of North Carolina, Wilmington; Lucien Frary, Rider University; Lydia Gerber, Washington State University; Erwin P. Grieshaber, Minnesota State University, Mankato; Russell D. Jones, Eastern Michigan University; Andrew J. Kirkendall, Texas A&M University; Elaine MacKinnon, University of West Georgia; Christopher Mauriello, Salem State College; Raphael Chijioke Njoku, University of Louisville; Michael J. Seth, James Madison University; Eric Swedin, Weber State University–Davis; and Michael G. Vann, Sacramento State University. At Bedford/St. Martin's, this project was in the safe hands of Mary Dougherty, Heidi Hood, Jennifer Jovin, Emily Berleth, and Andrew Ensor; Nancy Benjamin of Books By Design oversaw production from copyediting to final page proofs. Very special thanks to Sylvia Mallory for her superb, meticulous editorial work.

Padraic Kenney

Contents

Illustrations

PART ONE

Introduction: Causes, Comparisons, and Connections

In February 1986, two of the most stubborn dictators in the world, Ferdinand Marcos of the Philippines and Jean-Claude "Baby Doc" Duvalier of Haiti, suddenly found themselves out of power. The coincidence of these dramatic upheavals, each featuring joyous crowds, charismatic new leaders, and an apparent melting away of the instruments of repression, seemed to promise a fraying of dictatorship's hold on power everywhere. Indeed, within two years, the military dictatorship in Chile was on its way out, part of a general retreat of dictatorships in Latin America, from Argentina to Mexico. Then came the rapid exit from power of Communist leaders in Eastern Europe and the (soon to be former) Soviet Union. By the beginning of the 1990s, even some dictatorships in Africa, as well as the apartheid regime in South Africa, were giving way to new distributions of power.

Over a decade spanning the mid-1980s to the mid-1990s, a wave of political change swept across the globe. Some twenty to thirty countries underwent rapid democratization.[1] This trend was not universal; democracy movements in China and Burma (Myanmar), for example, were suppressed with bloodshed. In many parts of the world, especially in the countries of the former Soviet Union, the old elites reconsolidated their power under new ideological banners. Still, the shift toward democracy, which was both nonviolent and pluralistic, changed the relationship between the democratic and nondemocratic parts of

1

the world. Most fundamentally, democracy was no longer an attribute only of wealthy Western states, Japan, and India. Instead, it was a system to which the people of any country could realistically aspire.

Just as important, where once a dictatorship's end might be inconceivable without either intensive U.S. support or an armed struggle or both, now there was a new paradigm of grassroots change. Crowds mocked their leaders instead of calling for blood, making a point of refraining from violence. Social movements mobilized people around diverse yet practicable goals. Voters used elections to wrest power peacefully from dictators—and the dictators acquiesced. Further, opposition leaders recognized that one could gain more by talking to dictators than by killing them. It is true that the new paradigm could be as misleading as the old one. Belief in elections as the solution to all ills, and in the virtue of nonviolent change, is powerless against a dictator who is willing to use force; support from the streets could be window dressing for a new and equally repressive populist dictator. Nevertheless, the emergence of this belief in peaceful transformation is arguably the most novel development of all.

The revolutions at the end of the cold war—the post–World War II period of heightened tension between the United States and the Soviet Union—constitute one of the most important global realignments of the twentieth century. It is an era that has left its indelible imprint on our own time. Think of the use of the term *people power*, which is today invoked in writing about political change in Iraq, Thailand, Lebanon, and even the United States, but which caught the world's imagination in the Philippines in 1986. Consider the insistent attention to voting freedoms as a fundamental part of human rights. Arguments about the wisdom of "nation building" and "regime change" in the United States make implicit assumptions about how the regimes featured in this volume fell or retained power and about whether revolution is even possible.

The democratic revolutions in this book centered on one exemplary year: 1989. For those who believe in the power of numbers, 1989 is a stronger number than most. It was a year rich in anniversaries: two hundred years since the French Revolution, seventy years since a revolutionary movement introduced democracy to China, and twenty-one years since the last global upheaval, the student uprisings of 1968—a year whose last two digits, rotated upside down, revealed their successor. Such coincidences may seem trivial, but the power of numbers helps to account for the way 9/11 in the United States and 7/7 in Great Britain have come to symbolize the new terrorism.

Imagery is another reason that 1989 forms the symbolic heart of the era. Although we can look at a picture of a flag-waving crowd and have difficulty identifying the scene, we have no such trouble with images of people dancing atop a graffiti-covered concrete wall as they did in Berlin in November 1989. To be sure, those dancers did not themselves accomplish very much, and they certainly did not bring down a dictatorship, but their revelry vividly captured the spirit of that age. And the photographs and film footage from Eastern Europe that thrilled viewers in the United States were matched by similarly spirited images from Asia, Africa, and South America.

To a great extent, that spirit still inspires. We live, so we are often told, in a "post-9/11" world—but in fact, our world was first transformed by 1989. We need to be aware of that era and allow it to speak to us. Hence this book.

ORIGINS OF AN ERA

Two powerful types of factors underlie any great international event in the modern world. At closest range, there are singular individuals, both well known and obscure, who spur events in their own countries or who import or export them to new places. The documents in this book give voice to many such people. At greater remove, and equally important, are long-term or structural factors such as economic, social, and cultural trends and changes in political institutions. Without them, leaders and movements will be unlikely to find many followers or allies.

Four structural causes in particular deserve mention: generational change, technological advances, the emergence of human rights and nonviolence discourses, and the waning of the cold war.

Generational Change

In the historical sense, generations are created by shared dramatic events. Thus, for example, people who experienced World War II as their first major life crisis (those who were 18 to 30, perhaps, in 1945) might come to share certain perspectives on politics, among other things, that would not be shared by individuals older or younger than they. Another such generational gap emerged very strongly in 1968. That year, students and young workers across Europe and North America—people to whom the traumas of the war were both distant and frustratingly hidden—expressed frustration with their leaders' economic, cultural, and educational policies.[2] They argued that cold war political divisions, exemplified in the United States by the Vietnam War, caused enormous suffering to people in the third world for little gain, and they bemoaned the way that obsession with material goods had dulled affluent societies' sensitivity to social injustice. That rebellion of the late 1960s came roughly two decades after the end of World War II. After another two decades, the generational clock would again bring to the fore a generation dissatisfied with its predecessors' approach.

That 1968 generation in the West had been deeply interested in ideology and in the conflict between the right and the left. In a way, the members of the 1968 generation accepted the divisions of the cold war by embracing the other side—championing Communist leaders Mao Zedong of China or Ho Chi Minh of Vietnam, for example. Student and youth unrest stretched around the world, showing up, in very different manifestations, in Latin America, China, and the Soviet Bloc, as well as in Western Europe and the United States. The next generation, that of the 1980s, would produce its antithesis, which also emerged in multiple places at one time. Those who came of age in the 1980s constituted a generation that no longer had any adult memories of the ideological conflicts of the 1960s and early 1970s. They would question the need for ideological battles at all, and thus the need for violent overthrow of regimes. The antimaterialist or anticapitalist strain that was important to many in 1968 also had lost its urgency as a goal in itself (though it survives and has since reemerged in antiglobalization and environmental movements). These and other commonalities can be seen in democratic movements around the world in the 1980s.

Just as the '68ers owed much to thinkers of an older generation, so too there were many authorities from another older generation active in and around 1989. Ledivina Cariño (Document 16) and Fang Lizhi (Document 29), for example, demonstrate these intergenerational ties between students and professors. The democratic revolutions of the late cold war were in fact much less a revolt of youth than had been the upheavals of 1968. Still, generational change was one factor in the more recent era.

Technological Advances

A second factor in the revolutions of the late twentieth century was technological transformation, particularly in communications. In 1968, the one major communication technology of relevance was television. Broadcasts from Vietnam reached the developed world (at least), as did film footage of a Black Power protest by medal-winning U.S. athletes at the Olympic Games in Mexico City. Protesters at the Democratic National Convention in Chicago that August, however, had vastly overstated the case when they chanted, "The whole world is watching!" in protest of a violent police crackdown. Television, moreover, had been a passive means of communication and one then still lacking in choice. Consider, in contrast, the impact of cable television, satellite dishes, video cameras, videocassettes, cassette and microcassette recorders, fax machines, photocopiers, offset printers, and personal computers. All of these came into mass production after 1968; some owed their success to the development of the microprocessor in the early 1970s.

Just as often, however, relatively modest technological change could greatly boost the power of dissent in repressive countries. Protests by dissidents in Poland and the Philippines (Documents 10, 11, 13, and 15), for example, spread as a result of rapid printing technologies. In Chile, the opposition learned to subvert official broadcast media while also employing more traditional posters (Document 20) to get its message out. At the heart of all successful cases is the decentralization of control over, and production of, media. In China, by contrast, students were hampered in part by their inability to manipulate the still fully centralized media (see Document 30).

New technologies vastly increased the range of communication by opening up access to a greater variety of sources. Someone who could not get an original of a political manifesto might read a photocopy circulating in the underground. Another might find satellite news (including information not broadcast on state-run television) on a cable TV channel like CNN, which went worldwide in 1985. An opposition activist might use faxes to circumvent regime restrictions on communication.[3] Such technological advances also reduced costs in terms of both time and money: Photocopying, for example, was much more efficient than retyping a document or using carbon paper to make copies. Thus protest movements in the 1980s had much greater resources for mass communication at their disposal than did their predecessors. These revolutions, incidentally, occurred just before the advent of cell phones and the Internet, which would put much more communication power in the hands of ordinary people.

Increased access to technology is also a marker for a rising standard of living, and many scholars argue that the spread of wealth was an essential part of change: that people with a secure and rising income are much more likely to demand political rights than are the very poor. Political scientist Samuel Huntington, for example, has argued this point.[4] Yet economic development sometimes leads to a rise in standards of living *without* democracy, as in Singapore today. The case of

China, in this book, raises the question of whether the desire for democracy and the desire for prosperity are even compatible. Nor does relative poverty—the perception of being deprived in comparison to other countries—help to explain revolutionary movements. Protesters in the 1980s rarely talked about the economy, though Polish dissident Jacek Kuroń, South African activist Nelson Mandela, and Ukrainian politician Ivan Drach (Documents 12, 24, and 28), for example, each raise different kinds of economic concerns.

Technological progress might not have made as much difference without changes in the transportation of goods and people, as the VCR exemplifies. This technology had a double effect in the revolutions of the 1980s, as an object of desire and as a transmitter of messages. But it was only in the late 1980s that VCRs became widely available in Western Europe and East Asia, thanks to the spread of production into new areas, such as South Korea, where it had not been practical before. The growth of the shipping industry in the 1970s had much to do with the spread of manufacturing and the wider availability of electronic products. Only then could the Polish tourist returning from West Germany, or the Hong Kong resident visiting relatives in Shanghai, bring home such valuable and affordable goods.

Emergence of Discourse on Nonviolence and Human Rights

The medium did not make the message, however. The content of the message had also changed. Over the twentieth century, new ideas about opposition had been articulated. First, Mohandas Gandhi and others developed *nonviolence* as a response to repression. Nonviolence not only demonstrated moral superiority to the British control of India in the 1920s; it also proved to be devastatingly effective as long as a regime was hesitant to use total force. And while Gandhi emphasized Indian tradition as part of his strategy, Martin Luther King Jr. modernized and expanded the repertoire of nonviolent resistance. Both Gandhi and King had significant influence on the thinkers and movements in this book.[5]

Second, *human rights* became a force in international politics in the 1970s. Even a generation earlier, human rights issues had barely been on any international agenda, although they were not unheard of: The UN issued the Universal Declaration of Human Rights in 1948, and Amnesty International was founded in 1962. Yet the former was a document all too easily ignored, and the latter only began to have a significant impact in the late 1970s. The cold war had something to do with the neglect of human rights; almost until the end of that conflict, leaders of more powerful states (such as the United States and the Soviet Union) tended to place ideological rivalry ahead of human rights. Then when diplomats, among them the U.S. secretary of state, Henry Kissinger, turned aside from cold war ideology in the early 1970s, they embraced *realpolitik*, a pragmatic politics focused on national self-interest instead of ideological or moral concerns.

Ironically, these leaders themselves played an inadvertent role in putting human rights on the international agenda. A conference of European and North American diplomats at Helsinki, Finland, in 1974–1975 was meant to produce a document on security issues, such as borders and passports. But the Soviet delegation proposed that the assembled delegates also affirm recognition of basic human rights like freedom of speech and freedom to travel. At the time, Western acceptance of this proposal seemed to many like a caving-in to the Soviets. Yet Soviet Bloc dissidents seized on this document, ratified by their governments, as a contract of sorts. They formed "Helsinki committees" (sometimes using that name) to monitor human rights abuses in their countries. Their bravery in turn inspired U.S. human rights activists to form similar groups, first to monitor and support the work of their European colleagues (Helsinki Watch, founded in 1978). In the 1980s, this work expanded to the Americas (America Watch, 1981), Asia (1985), Africa (1988), and the Middle East (1989).

By the early 1980s, then, in much the same way as *globalization* has become a buzzword in international politics today, so too human rights entered the lexicon everywhere. Even if these rights were not universally respected (as they still are not), their articulation and general recognition meant that, much more than before, ordinary people became a constituency to be considered in international relations. Access to information, justice, security, and acceptable living standards could now become substantive issues in the international arena. U.S. president Jimmy Carter, as well as nongovernmental organizations like those mentioned earlier, played a significant role in ensuring that the issue of human rights would now affect relations between states.

End of the Cold War

In all of the cases we examine in this book, Communist parties and their powerful patrons in Moscow or Beijing played a key role. In some instances, the Communists were directly in charge, and no one could imagine their being dislodged without violence or even another world war. In other cases, it was the U.S. fear of communism that helped to keep local dictators in charge. Communist parties and guerrilla movements remained strong in many places in Asia, Latin America, and Africa. They depended in part on a touchstone to which they could all refer: the vitality of the parent ideology in the Soviet Union and China. Leaders of these countries produced powerful revolutionary rhetoric that continued to inspire millions; they also provided invaluable assistance (arms, publications, and advisers) to comrades throughout the world.

The cold war did not end until 1991, when the Soviet Union fragmented. Yet by that time, most of the countries profiled in this book had already completed their democratic revolutions or were well on their way. It would be inaccurate, then, to identify the end of hostilities between the two world superpowers as a cause of democratic change. Communism had already begun to decline as a dynamic force in world politics in the mid-1970s, however. Mao Zedong (born 1893) died in 1976; his successor, Deng Xiaoping, soon began to scale back the revolutionary ambitions of Chinese communism. In the Soviet Union, Leonid Brezhnev (born 1906) died senile in 1982; three years later, Mikhail Gorbachev took the reins of the Communist party and attempted to reform and rescue the Soviet regime (Document 7). Although their respective regimes continued to support Communist revolutionaries (such as in the Philippines, Chile, and South Africa) and other Communist regimes, the aim of Communist world domination became increasingly unrealistic. In turn, authoritarian leaders who had in part staked their control on the fear of communism lost an argument for maintaining their grip on power.

The first meeting between Gorbachev and U.S. president Ronald Reagan took place in Geneva, Switzerland, in November 1985. Three months later, Reagan reluctantly relinquished his belief that Philippine dictator Ferdinand Marcos was an essential bulwark against the Communist threat. Soon, Chilean leader General Augusto Pinochet, who had come to power with U.S. support, would become equally dispensable. Reagan's successor, George H. W. Bush, would continue this policy of acquiescence to democratic transformation. Both presidents found a once-familiar world changing rapidly.

THE CONTOURS OF A REVOLUTIONARY WAVE

The stage was now set, as a result of the several factors just discussed, for the democratic revolutions. What were the chief features of this era? Several of them were hinted at earlier and now deserve a closer look.

Nonviolence

A key uniting feature of all the revolutions was nonviolence. Several of the causes of 1989 discussed earlier are relevant here. Advances in communication technologies, for example, clearly gave new kinds of weapons to regime opponents. Although dissidents could certainly use a photocopier to incite an armed rebellion, the newfound ability to reach masses of people took away some of the need for violence. Violent uprisings, after all, are more likely if the opposition perceives itself to be outnumbered; new technologies drew in larger numbers of supporters and heightened the ruling powers' awareness of those numbers. The exception of China illustrates this point: The hunger strikers in Document 31, while peaceful, speak of sacrificing their lives, and Chai Ling, in Document 32, implies that blood must be shed to attract attention and support. The peacefulness of the successful revolutions is all the more remarkable in the context of more violent uprisings elsewhere at the same time, such as the Iranian Revolution of 1979 (see Document 4) and the first Palestinian *intifada*, which began in 1987.[6]

Pluralism

The new revolutionaries were also pluralist. That is, they did not, for the most part, assert one correct political program but instead conceded that there might be many different approaches. They did not seek to impose one political vision but rather a framework within which many ideas, political or otherwise, might flourish. The waning of ideological allegiances that accompanied the cold war's decline also figured in the nonviolence. The movements documented in this book were revolutionary without espousing revolutionary ideologies as usually understood. Thus, whereas one might be ready to kill for the victory of the proletariat over the capitalists, could one do the same for democracy?

Transnationality

The wave of revolutions can be called a *transnational moment*, a period of heightened awareness of events and trends in other countries. Gorbachev's visit to Beijing in May 1989, for example, inspired Chinese students who had been following events in Eastern Europe and the Soviet Union. In the Philippines, many were aware that resistance to dictatorship had emerged in similarly Catholic Poland six years earlier. In South Africa, political prisoners on Robben Island debated the import of the Solidarity movement, Poland's oppositional trade union, in their jail cells. When such a broad transmission of information occurs, we cannot be sure how the recipients interpret what they learn. Still, these influences, and the structural factors we considered earlier, account for the similar ways in which the authors of the documents discuss ideas of democracy, human rights, and personal responsibility. Meanwhile, international institutions—Western parliaments, universities, churches, and supranational bodies like the United Nations—encouraged or helped opposition movements while imposing sanctions on dictatorships. Before the widespread advocacy of human rights in the 1970s, such actions had been much more limited.

Deliberate, Explicable Change

Perhaps the most important aspect of the revolutions of the 1989 era was one that they share with other such moments, such as 1968: They were deliberate and explicable. The fact that the change was not sudden contradicts the common misperception that democratic revolutions are abrupt breaks. This mistaken notion is neatly captured in newspaper headlines and journalists' narratives that speak of "miracles." The term *people power*, which was widely used in the Philippines and Eastern Europe, also implies that the revolutions were disorganized, the result of a precipitous unleashing of people's elemental desires.

This "magical" characterization of the revolutions does a disservice to participants in revolutions that were well organized. Perhaps it reflects a natural desire on the part of observers to imagine themselves suddenly doing the right thing against great odds. We might call this perspective the "Rosa Parks syndrome" after the legendary U.S. civil rights activist who died in 2005. Tributes to Parks before and after her death often depicted her as an ordinary, tired lady who simply decided one day in 1954 that she would not get up and move to the back of the bus. She was thus one of us, the legend went, going about her business until suddenly she could not take it any more. In fact, Rosa Parks was anything but an unexpected, unlikely activist. Before her famous act of protest, she had been active in the civil rights movement for well over a decade, in both the NAACP and the Voters' League. There was no miracle of transformation here but the hard work of longtime activism in a persecuted social movement.

The same is true of the revolutions examined in this book. Lech Wałęsa, the electrician-turned-Solidarity-leader in Poland; Corazon

Aquino, the grieving-widow-turned-presidential-candidate in the Philippines; Wei Jingsheng, another electrician, whose writings sent him to a Chinese prison in 1978—each has been portrayed as an unlikely hero thrust suddenly into the limelight, swept away by the spirit of unforeseen popular protest. They are the Rosa Parkses of their revolutions. Yet in fact, each of them, and hundreds of others, came to the world's attention after years of struggle. Wałęsa was already a recognized worker activist in 1970; Aquino began thinking about her role in national politics when her husband, Benigno, was assassinated in 1983; Wei was a well-educated member of the Communist youth elite before the turmoil of Mao's Cultural Revolution forced him to rethink his position. These histories do not mean that any one of these individuals was ready for revolution, as perhaps no one can ever be prepared for such radical change; but it does mean that we do not need to invoke miracles, or simple human psychology, to explain their actions.

Social Movements as Catalysts of Change

The long-term causes we examined earlier help to explain how change could emerge in so many places at the same time: why popular critiques of different regimes are similar and why the proposed remedies may resemble one another. Moving from ideas to action, however, requires local, place-specific intervention. The key to this step is social movements, that is, organized groups engaged in collective action aimed toward political (or other) change. The crucial word here is *organized*. It may be hard for a reader in a democracy to imagine what groups of people working in secret against a repressive regime can do. Adam Michnik (Document 9) explores the role of an underground. Many other documents portray carefully planned actions, such as the outdoor meeting in Document 27, the play in Document 17, and the boycott in Document 15. In another example, Document 10 shows both the leaflet that summoned a crowd to a city square in Poland in June 1987 and the course of the subsequent demonstration. Spontaneity has its place, too, as in Document 23, but it is not a major feature of the democratic revolutions that are the subject of this volume, and "people power" more accurately refers to the way that social movements channel or enact political ideas.

How do small groups of committed activists engender revolution? The dislike that many people feel for bad regimes is not sufficient to explain their motivations. In truth, discontent may fester for decades in any country. In democracies, most discontent finds an outlet in legal ways of affecting the political system, its institutions, and their policies. In contrast, in authoritarian systems, such channels are at least partially blocked, yet popular discontent does not necessarily lead to revolutionary change. Most people prefer to avoid political contestation and in fact come to terms with repressive regimes, whether because they hope to protect their own families or their own aspirations from harm or because they discover that there are worthwhile gains to be had from making peace or even collaborating with the system. It is difficult, moreover, for most people to imagine a different system. Democracy may be inarguably better, but its appeal is not obvious to someone living in a dictatorship, any more than people living in a democracy can imagine living in a theocracy like Iran, for example, or in a concentration camp.

Political thinkers play a key role in breaking through people's indifference to change. See, for example, how Fang Lizhi (Document 29) and Nelson Mandela (Document 24) confront the problem of individuals' taking actions that support the regime to the detriment of fellow citizens. Such thinkers begin by analyzing the system in which they live. They ask: What are the fundamentals of this regime? Is the system alien or natural to us? What is right or wrong with the political vision that it advances? On what basis does this regime continue to rule, and how does it exercise power? Who are its supporters? Which rights do we have, and which have been taken away from us? Then they proceed to offer strategies of resistance, as well as values around which resistance can be organized. Nonviolence, pluralism, and human rights are common threads in democratic thought in the late 1970s and early 1980s.

WHOM WERE THEY FIGHTING?

Dictatorships were a common feature of world politics in the 1970s. In the quarter-century following World War II, more than fifty countries had gained their freedom in Africa, Asia, and the Caribbean, but few had established stable democratic governments. Moreover, the revolts of 1968 had not made the world any freer. Political systems on either side of the cold war barrier remained entrenched. But the existing dictatorships were of various kinds, and as these differences influenced the directions of change in the 1980s, a brief overview will be helpful.[7]

Communist Dictatorships

Communist dictatorships controlled all countries of Eastern Europe. Though independent, these countries were clearly subservient in foreign relations and economic policy, and to a lesser extent in internal affairs, to the Soviet Union. The leader of the Soviet Union, Leonid Brezhnev, had shown his determination to control Eastern European politics by invading Czechoslovakia in 1968 to crush the democratization movement known as the "Prague Spring." In 1979, he invaded Afghanistan to assert further the Soviet Union's right to ensure that its neighbors were one-party states. Indeed, the most important feature of Communist dictatorships was the role of the party and of the ideology that the party represented and defended. That ideology shaped what people learned in school, read or heard in the media, and were allowed to express. Through a system known as *nomenklatura*, the Communist party ensured that only trusted, trained, and obedient people would fill positions from prime minister down to elementary school principal. Except in the harshest regimes, such as Albania, terror was not a central tool of late Communist regimes; some governments, including those of Yugoslavia and Poland, allowed limited travel to other countries, some freedom of worship, and some artistic freedom. But the state (and behind it, the party) still controlled nearly every workplace and every cultural product.

Broadly, this description also fitted non-European Communist regimes like those of Cuba, China, North Korea, and Vietnam. Indeed, it is difficult to point to significant differences between these regimes and their European counterparts. The ideology might be flavored differently due to different religious traditions or social structure, but the practices—sometimes harsher, sometimes less so—were largely the same. Other regimes, such as in Burma and Ethiopia, used the language of communism but in a more opportunistic way: They were personal or military dictatorships that adopted the form and style of communism as part of an effort to gain aid from China and the Soviet Union, their wealthier ideological allies.

Militarized and Populist Dictatorships

In Latin America and parts of East and Southeast Asia, a different type of dictatorship, militarized and populist in nature, held sway. These regimes included Ferdinand Marcos's Philippines, Suharto's Indonesia, Reza Shah Pahlavi's Iran, Augusto Pinochet's Chile, and many others. Because they were for the most part not born of social revolution, they did not have at their base the drive to transform society, yet they were no less bloody for all that. In most cases, control was in the hands of the military or individual military leaders. Such dictatorships are generally less interested in transforming society because they have no guiding ideology. Instead, they position themselves *against* the disorder of democratic politics and social activism.

One common theme justifying both the seizure of power and continued repression in such dictatorships is the need for cleansing and for order, with leaders often claiming to be following the people's will. These regimes have killed, imprisoned, deprived of chosen livelihoods, or driven into exile millions of people. Militarized dictatorships (which in practice fall on the right side of the political ledger) have enjoyed the support of Western governments, the United States in particular, because they in turn tend to be tolerant of activities that do not threaten them in any way or that may help them remain in power (in contrast, more ideologically activist regimes often do things that weaken them—think of Adolf Hitler's annihilation of European Jews). In particular, such dictatorships tend to favor private enterprise and a semi-free market. But while many Western politicians at the time argued that right-wing dictatorships brought stability and economic development, those benefits were not obvious to the victims of those regimes.[8]

Although economic reform generally fitted easily into the goals of the military or populist dictatorships, political reform was by definition impossible because the core goal of the dictators was simply to maintain their own power. They used mass appeal and nationalism to mask a program of leader-worship. Another dark side of these regimes was massive corruption; Transparency International has estimated that Suharto was the most corrupt leader in recent history, having embezzled some $15 to 35 billion, with Marcos a distant second, having made off with $5 to 10 billion.[9] Communist regimes also saw a great deal of corruption, albeit smaller by at least an order of magnitude; in theory, however, they were reformable. That is, one could posit that the system itself could be improved, usually by returning to the basic principles on which the regimes had been founded. Instead of reform, which never did come close to success, European communism ended with revolution.

The Apartheid State

A third type of dictatorship is what one might call a "repressive democracy." This model is represented in this book by apartheid-era

South Africa, an example that often becomes a point of comparison in analyses of the restrictive measures employed by democracies like the United States, Britain, and Israel. In South Africa, a white minority enjoyed most of the freedoms of democracy, while the black majority was denied these freedoms. As Desmond Tutu (Document 3) and Nelson Mandela (Document 24) recognize, overcoming apartheid would require that both the privileged and those without any rights stand up to the established order.

All of these different types of regimes—Communist, militarized/populist, and apartheid—discovered in the 1980s that their hold on power was not as secure as it had once been. Their nationalist, moral, or ideological arguments for maintaining repressive power faded, in part because the opposition was able to articulate counterarguments. We can see this effort in documents as diverse as Gabriel Valdés's speech (Document 19) and Adam Michnik's letter from prison (Document 9). Meanwhile, the power of television, the rise of international human rights groups, and the development of concepts of nonviolent protest meant that violent, bloody repression of opposition came to seem a less viable option. As the Chinese exception will show, this factor could be decisive in enabling a revolution to take its course. Yet often enough, leaders needed to be persuaded (by foreign diplomats, by their own advisers, or by popular, organized protests) that they could not rely on force any longer.

THE PATHS TOWARD REVOLUTION

Some analysts, among them Indian-born U.S. journalist Fareed Zakaria, have argued that certain societies or cultures are more prepared for democratic change than others, thanks to economic success or cultural traditions. The question of whether democracy fits some societies and not others is probably one of the most vital of our century; much of U.S. foreign policy in the post–cold war era rests on assumptions about whether societies (in East, South, and Central Asia or in the Middle East, for example) are or can be made suitable for democracy. This cultural determinism—that is, the assumption that democratic practices are too deeply tied to Western culture to adapt to new environs in the foreseeable future—can be partially tested with the evidence of the documents that follow. Is Aung San Suu Kyi's advocacy of democracy and human rights (Document 6) as carefully argued and as deeply felt as Václav Havel's (Document 1)? Are the Polish social movements as open to alternative points of view as are the Chilean movements?

Certain long-term structural changes account partially for the worldwide scale of democratic protest in the late twentieth century. If we move to a middle level of analysis, we can separate out three distinct trends with regional effects, which in turn lead us to the decisive words and actions of individuals in each case examined in the body of this book:

- *Decolonization in Africa.* The first of these middle-level trends was a new phase in the decolonization of Africa. Though the bulk of the continent had won its freedom by the mid-1960s, one colonial power in particular, Portugal, had held out. Ultimately, however, the success of a democratic revolution there in 1974[10] led in short order to the independence of Portugal's southern African colonies of Angola and Mozambique. The probability then grew that their neighbor Rhodesia would fall, too.

  For over a decade, Rhodesia—where European settlers had declared independence from Britain in 1965 to stave off African rule—was the object of nearly universal opprobrium. Even the South African press doubted that white rule could survive against a much larger black insurgency and international isolation. When Rhodesian prime minister Ian Smith was forced to give up power in 1980, pressure increased on his new exile home, South Africa. Desmond Tutu took note of this connection in a speech in 1980 (Document 3). In turn, the fall of apartheid in South Africa had an undoubted influence on democratic movements elsewhere on the continent, such as in Mozambique and Nigeria.

- *Corruption on high and economic power in Asia and South America.* A second pattern emerged in Asia and South America. In Asia, the threat of communism and the concomitant U.S. desire to maintain a strong military presence had contributed to decades of military dictatorships, from South Korea to Thailand. It was probably a combination of the incredible levels of corruption at the top and growing economic power from below that began to weaken these regimes—and U.S. reliance on them—even before the end of the cold war. The Philippine revolution was the first in a still-incomplete chain, which continued on through political change in South Korea, Taiwan, Thailand, and Indonesia. Some of the same factors, meanwhile, account for the weakening of dictatorships in South America at about the same time. Changing patterns of U.S. support for dictators were especially important. Chile, the major example of such shifting support, has experienced the most lasting democratic revolution. Most Latin American countries have experienced some political upheaval in the last two decades. In recent years, democracies in the region have found that U.S. ties, and the accompanying market liberalization, can be a liability that leads to new pressures from political movements representing the impoverished.

- *Communism's fall in Europe.* Finally, the fall of communism in Europe is the central story at the cold war's end. The story bears some similarities to the end of apartheid because in both cases an ideological system that was above any one leader crumbled even as economic stagnation and foreign pressures played a role. The end of communism is traceable to various points: the election of Gorbachev in 1985, the founding of Solidarity in Poland in 1980 (Document 8), and perhaps the Helsinki Accords of 1975, discussed earlier.

  This story is in fact multicentered in that its effects also ranged most widely, as the declining fear of communism weakened the raison d'être of authoritarian regimes around the world. Two cases from the fall of communism—Poland and Ukraine—appear in this book because the revolutions in Eastern Europe in 1989, represented here by Poland, differed in significant ways from the breakup of the Soviet Union two years later, which produced an independent Ukraine. While most of Eastern Europe is now firmly within the democratic and prosperous sphere of the European Union, Ukraine and its former Soviet neighbors remain uncertain of that country's future.

These regional strands were initially separate and distinct. However, at about the same time, they converged in a common set of patterns—critiques of power, social movements, and nonviolent revolution.

A WORD ABOUT COMPARATIVE HISTORY

Taking note of these various factors, the reader may still wonder, upon approaching the cases in this book, how much background knowledge is necessary to analyze them. Even an experienced historian might know just one or two of these countries well, so it is reasonable to ask how one can make sense of six cases.

Comparative history, however, works from the assumption that we can use models, structural factors, and analogies to approach the unfamiliar. This approach allows us to gain from seeing with fresh eyes what is before us. Reading a collection of documents on any one country, we can and should ask ourselves what contexts are missing. But we should not assume that we need to gather more background because our assumptions about what is important may be quite wrong. For example, we might know that most Poles are Catholic and that the Chinese honor Confucian traditions, or that Chile and the Philippines were once part of the Spanish Empire. But it does not follow that such information is relevant in studying their late–cold war revolutions or that it will be relevant in the way we expect. When making a new acquaintance, we are likely to begin by thinking about what we see and hear directly rather than inquiring about his or her upbringing or religious beliefs; we can use the same approach with unfamiliar societies. The task of comparative work is not to gather ever-deeper knowledge about the cases in question but to draw connections by using the available information.

CONCLUSION

It remains to discuss the very terminology of *revolution* that appears in the title of this book. Many observers have instead chosen to apply the term *transition* or *reform* to the events of the 1980s and 1990s that we will examine.[11] To them, the word *revolution* connotes violence, catharsis, and the destruction of society, the economy, and the state. According to this interpretation, revolutions are also supposed to give rise to new forms of politics and culture. The changes under consideration in this book, these analysts would argue, were largely nonviolent and did not produce new types of government or radical cultural experiments. Indeed, the old elites were not slaughtered but were allowed to leave, to retire, or even to remain in Parliament. Some have even returned to power, although they have tended to respect the postrevolutionary system. None of this sounds like the revolutions of the past.

Yet the events documented in this book moved with the dramatic pace that we associate with revolution and did have a fundamental impact on the economy, the political system, and even the social structure in their respective countries. Disenfranchised people gained rights, creative (economic, social, and sometimes cultural) forces were unleashed, and the doors were thrown open to the pursuit of hidden information. Regimes that had come to seem nearly permanent melted away, and people organized themselves in new ways almost overnight. What is not revolutionary about such a course of events?

How we evaluate the revolutions that occurred at the cold war's conclusion has continuing political relevance. Many American politicians, for example, accept the idea that U.S. military might and political leadership caused the downfall of the Communist adversary. Although in truth these were not a major factor at all, this belief certainly contributed to the belief that the same set of factors would result in the transformation of the Middle East, beginning in Afghanistan in 2001.

Encountering the revolutions of the cold war's end should lead to new conclusions about what political change in our time looks like and what prevents such change. To reach such conclusions, one must analyze the evidence, and that is the task of readers of this book.

NOTES

[1] Most analysts draw on the annual publication *Freedom in the World: Political Rights and Civil Liberties*, published by Freedom House, to make such an estimate. See also Adrian Karatnycky and Peter Ackerman, *How Freedom Is Won: From Civic Resistance to Durable Democracy* (New York: Freedom House, 2005). An exact number is impossible, as it depends on one's choice of parameters, such as the speed and depth of change.

[2] For a survey of the forces shaping 1968, see Gerd-Rainer Horn, *The Spirit of '68: Rebellion in Western Europe and North America, 1956–1976* (Oxford: Oxford University Press, 2007); and Arthur Marwick, *The Sixties: Cultural Revolution in Britain, France, Italy and the United States, c. 1958–c. 1974* (Oxford: Oxford University Press, 1998).

[3] The fax machine played a critical role in resistance to the coup in the Soviet Union in August 1991. See Ann Cooper, "The Foreign Press and the Coup," in *Eyewitness Accounts of the August 1991 Coup*, ed. Victoria E. Bonnell, Ann Cooper, and Gregory Freidin, 308–17 (Armonk, N.Y.: M. E. Sharpe, 1994).

[4] Samuel Huntington, *The Third Wave: Democratization in the Late Twentieth Century* (Norman: University of Oklahoma Press, 1991), 60–63.

[5] See Peter Ackerman and Jack DuVall, *A Force More Powerful: A Century of Nonviolent Conflict* (New York: St. Martin's, 2000); and Jonathan Schell, *The Unconquerable World: Power, Nonviolence and the Will of the People* (New York: Holt, 2004). When I conducted interviews with participants in Eastern European social movements, activists in nearly every country recalled the impact of Richard Attenborough's film *Gandhi*,

televised in the mid-1980s. Frequently, they characterized King's struggle as more comparable to their own.

[6]See Mary Elizabeth King, *A Quiet Revolution: The First Palestinian Intifada and Nonviolent Resistance* (New York: Nation Books, 2007).

[7]Scholars still debate whether these regimes could be called "totalitarian" (implying desire, partially realized, to control and remake everything) or "authoritarian" (emphasizing maintenance of power rather than the forced transformation of society and individuals). A useful summary is Paul Brooker, *Non-Democratic Regimes: Theory, Government, and Politics* (New York: Palgrave Macmillan, 2000), chap. 1.

[8]See David F. Schmitz, *The United States and Right-Wing Dictatorships, 1965–1989* (Cambridge: Cambridge University Press, 2006).

[9]Transparency International, *Global Corruption Report, 2004*, available at www.transparency.org.

[10]The democratic transformations in Mediterranean Europe—Spain, Portugal, and Greece—in the mid-1970s did have some effect on the revolutions a decade later. Besides the impact of Portugal's decolonization, one could also point to the demonstration effect of those three countries' gaining admission to the European Community in the 1980s.

[11]Timothy Garton Ash coined the term *refolution* in his book *The Magic Lantern: The Revolution of '89, Witnessed in Warsaw, Budapest, Berlin, and Prague* (New York: Random House, 1990), suggesting that these were hybrid events, more than reform but not quite revolution.

PART TWO

The Documents

1

New Ideas of Democracy and Dissent

Philosophers and politicians have been thinking and writing about democracy and the paths toward democracy for a very long time. However, while the words used might remain the same, the content changes. The documents in this chapter illustrate some of the strands of new thinking that emerged in the 1970s and 1980s, contributing to the strategies of the era's democratic movements. The writings reflect their time period in several ways. First, the authors tend not to see the world in black and white, and they do not demonize their opponents. Each writer has seen his or her country torn apart by horrific violence that has taken thousands, even millions, of lives. They search for ways in which people can take control of their political destinies without harming others. Second, talk of human rights as a basis and goal of the democratic struggle was still relatively new in the 1970s. All of the documents that follow draw attention to the rights of individuals and groups in society. They also use moral arguments to justify the need for political change. Whether as religious leaders, politicians, philosophers, or scholars, all invoke moral themes, such as personal conscience and responsibility, in some way.

There are also important distinctions among the documents. Where some assert, directly or indirectly, the need to reform existing institutions, others entirely reject the regime's institutions or call for their radical renewal. Thus, too, some call for collective action, while others speak to what individuals can and should do. For some of the authors, change is inevitable and the regime they oppose is doomed, while for others the need for action is urgent.

The documents in this chapter come from Czechoslovakia, China, South Africa, Iran, Chile, Burma, and the Soviet Union. They do not lead us directly to the documents in the subsequent chapters' case studies, though three are from those countries. Instead, they allow the reader to build a vocabulary of political change, which can then be tested against the specific cases.

In reading these documents, each time the word *democracy* is used—or *moral* or *people* or *freedom* or other key words—consider what the writer means by the term. Look at adjacent words or phrases for clues. Consider the differing belief systems (Communist, Socialist, Islamic, Buddhist, Christian) that may shape the writers' thoughts.

Also ask yourself: How does each author conceptualize the regime? Is the system considered intransigent? A partner in dialogue? Susceptible to pressure? Where does change come from, and how much power does the individual have to bring about change? Finally, does the writer offer a concrete plan of action, or is the document instead meant to provoke reflection?

1

VÁCLAV HAVEL

The Power of the Powerless

1978

Václav Havel (1936–) is a Czech playwright who became famous as one of the spokespersons of the group Charter 77, founded in Prague in January 1977 to call the Communists to account for their violations of human rights. Havel wrote "The Power of the Powerless" after a clandestine meeting of Czech, Slovak, and Polish dissidents on the mountain border between the two countries. In the essay, he seeks to understand just how the Communist regimes incapacitate people politically and whether people can free themselves. Even though ordinary citizens appear powerless, he argues, the regime's need for their passive consent—he portrays a shopkeeper mindlessly placing Communist slogans in his shop window to commemorate official holidays—gives them great subversive power. He calls on people to "live within the truth," to live according to their own sense of responsibility, and not to accept the falsehoods of the Communist system. In this excerpt, he introduces the figure of the dissident and shows how "independent life" can emerge naturally, parallel to that which the Com-

From Václav Havel, "The Power of the Powerless," in *Open Letters: Selected Writings, 1965–1990*, ed. Paul Wilson (New York: Vintage, 1992), 174–79, 192–96.

munists control. With the fall of communism in 1989, Havel was elected president of Czechoslovakia.

You do not become a "dissident" just because you decide one day to take up this most unusual career. You are thrown into it by your personal sense of responsibility, combined with a complex set of external circumstances. You are cast out of the existing structures and placed in a position of conflict with them. It begins as an attempt to do your work well and ends with being branded an enemy of society. . . .

If what I have called living within the truth is a basic existential (and of course potentially political) starting point for all those "independent citizens' initiatives" and "dissident" or "opposition" movements this does not mean that every attempt to live within the truth automatically belongs in this category. On the contrary, in its most original and broadest sense, living within the truth covers a vast territory whose outer limits are vague and difficult to map, a territory full of modest expressions of human volition, the vast majority of which will remain anonymous and whose political impact will probably never be felt or described any more concretely than simply as a part of a social climate or mood. Most of these expressions remain elementary revolts against manipulation: you simply straighten your backbone and live in greater dignity as an individual.

Here and there—thanks to the nature, the assumptions, and the professions of some people, but also thanks to a number of accidental circumstances such as the specific nature of the local milieu, friends, and so on—a more coherent and visible initiative may emerge from this wide and anonymous hinterland, an initiative that transcends "merely" individual revolt and is transformed into more conscious, structured, and purposeful work. The point where living within the truth ceases to be a mere negation of living with a lie and becomes articulate in a particular way is the point at which something is born that might be called the "independent spiritual, social, and political life of society." This independent life is not separated from the rest of life ("dependent life") by some sharply defined line. Both types frequently co-exist in the same people. Nevertheless, its most important focus is marked by a relatively high degree of inner emancipation. It sails upon the vast ocean of the manipulated life like little boats, tossed by the waves but always bobbing back as visible messengers of living within the truth, articulating the suppressed aims of life. . . .

Thus what will later be referred to as "citizens' initiatives," "dissident movements," or even "oppositions," emerge, like the proverbial one tenth of the iceberg visible above the water, from that area, from the independent life of society. In other words, just as the independent life of society develops out of living within the truth in the widest sense of the word, as the distinct, articulated expression of that life, so "dissent" gradually emerges from the independent life of society. . . .

What follows from this description? Nothing more and nothing less than this: it is impossible to talk about what in fact "dissidents" do and the effect of their work without first talking about the work of all those who, in one way or another, take part in the independent life of society and who are not necessarily "dissidents" at all. They may be writers who write as they wish without regard for censorship or official demands and who issue their work—when official publishers refuse to print it—as *samizdat*.[1] They may be philosophers, historians, sociologists, and all those who practice independent scholarship and, if it is impossible through official or semi-official channels, who also circulate their work in *samizdat* or who organize private discussions, lectures, and seminars. They may be teachers who privately teach young people things that are kept from them in the state schools; clergymen who either in office or, if they are deprived of their charges, outside it, try to carry on a free religious life; painters, musicians, and singers who practice their work regardless of how it is looked upon by official institutions; everyone who shares this independent culture and helps to spread it; people who, using the means available to them, try to express and defend the actual social interests of workers, to put real meaning back into trade unions or to form independent ones; people who are not afraid to call the attention of officials to cases of injustice and who strive to see that the laws are observed; and the different groups of young people who try to extricate themselves from manipulation and live in their own way, in the spirit of their own hierarchy of values. The list could go on.

. . . If living within the truth is an elementary starting point for every attempt made by people to oppose the alienating pressure of the system, if it is the only meaningful basis of any independent act of political import, and if, ultimately, it is also the most intrinsic existential source of the "dissident" attitude, then it is difficult to imagine that even manifest "dissent" could have any other basis than the service of

[1] *samizdat* (literally, "self-published"): underground literature.

truth, the truthful life, and the attempt to make room for the genuine aims of life. . . .

If the basic job of the "dissident" movements is to serve truth, that is, to serve the real aims of life, and if that necessarily develops into a defense of individuals and their right to a free and truthful life (that is, a defense of human rights and a struggle to see the laws respected), then another stage of this approach, perhaps the most mature stage so far, is what Václav Benda[2] called the development of "parallel structures." . . .

What are these structures? . . . The term *second culture* very rapidly came to be used for the whole area of independent and repressed culture, that is, not only for art and its various currents but also for the humanities, the social sciences, and philosophical thought. This second culture, quite naturally, has created elementary organizational forms: *samizdat* editions of books and magazines, private performances and concerts, seminars, exhibitions, and so on. . . . [There are] potential or embryonic forms of such structures in other spheres as well: from a parallel information network to parallel forms of education (private universities), parallel trade unions, parallel foreign contacts, to a kind of hypothesis on a parallel economy. On the basis of these parallel structures, [Benda] then develops the notion of a "parallel *polis*" or state or, rather, he sees the rudiments of such a *polis* in these structures.

At a certain stage in its development, the independent life of society and the "dissident" movements cannot avoid a certain amount of organization and institutionalization. This is a natural development, and unless this independent life of society is somehow radically suppressed and eliminated, the tendency will grow. Along with it, a parallel political life will also necessarily evolve, and to a certain extent it exists already in Czechoslovakia. Various groupings of a more or less political nature will continue to define themselves politically, to act and confront each other.

These parallel structures, it may be said, represent the most articulated expressions so far of living within the truth. One of the most important tasks the "dissident" movements have set themselves is to support and develop them. Once again, it confirms the fact that all attempts by society to resist the pressure of the system have their essential beginnings in the "pre-political" area. For what else are parallel structures than an area where a different life can be lived, a life

---

[2] *Václav Benda* (1946–1999): Czech political activist, participant in Charter 77.

that is in harmony with its own aims and which in turn structures itself in harmony with those aims? What else are those initial attempts at social self-organization than the efforts of a certain part of society to live—as a society—within the truth, to rid itself of the self-sustaining aspects of totalitarianism and, thus, to extricate itself radically from its involvement in the post-totalitarian system? What else is it but a nonviolent attempt by people to negate the system within themselves and to establish their lives on a new basis, that of their own proper identity? And does this tendency not confirm once more the principle of returning the focus to actual individuals? After all, the parallel structures do not grow *a priori* out of a theoretical vision of systemic changes (there are no political sects involved), but from the aims of life and the authentic needs of real people. In fact, all eventual changes in the system, changes we may observe here in their rudimentary forms, have come about as it were *de facto*, from "below," because life compelled them to, not because they came before life, somehow directing it or forcing some change on it.

... Patočka[3] used to say that the most interesting thing about responsibility is that we carry it with us everywhere. That means that responsibility is ours, that we must accept it and grasp it here, now, in this place in time and space where the Lord has set us down, and that we cannot lie our way out of it by moving somewhere else, whether it be to an Indian ashram or to a parallel *polis*. . . .

In other words, the parallel *polis* points beyond itself and makes sense only as an act of deepening one's responsibility to and for the whole, as a way of discovering the most appropriate *locus* for this responsibility, not as an escape from it.

---

[3]*Jan Patočka* (1907–1977): Czech philosopher, one of the founders of Charter 77. He died as a result of his treatment at the hands of the secret police.

2

WEI JINGSHENG

The Fifth Modernization: Democracy

December 1978

Wei Jingsheng (1950–) experienced communism quite differently than Havel, having never lived under another political system. His youth was marked by participation as a Red Guard, a militant young enthusiast in Mao Zedong's Cultural Revolution, the destructive, chaotic campaign of the late 1960s. Yet he came to reconsider his enthusiasm for communism and welcomed the thaw that followed Mao's death in 1976.

In December 1978, Mao's successor, Deng Xiaoping, promoted the need for Four Modernizations in agriculture, industry, science and technology, and national defense. Wei, then an electrician at the Beijing Zoo, responded immediately by posting the essay excerpted below as a poster on the Democracy Wall, a brick wall in Beijing's old city. At first, the authorities encouraged postings on this wall, hoping that they would help to discredit political opponents while providing support for China's transformation. Wei Jingsheng argues in this essay that Deng's modernization is incomplete without the empowerment of the people. Though he was no longer a Communist, Wei's essay shows that he is still suspicious of capitalism and believes in the role of workers. Nevertheless, his poster essay landed him in prison for almost fifteen years.

What is democracy? True democracy means placing all power in the hands of the working people. Are working people unable to manage state power? Yugoslavia has taken this route and proven to us that people have no need for dictators, whether big or small; they can take care of things much better themselves.[1]

[1] Communist Yugoslavia at this time had a system of "socialist self-management," in which many economic decisions were made by workers' councils at the factory level rather than by government ministers and factory managers.

From Wei Jingsheng, "The Fifth Modernization: Democracy," in Wei Jingsheng, *The Courage to Stand Alone: Letters from Prison and Other Writings*, ed. and trans. Kristina M. Torgeson (New York: Penguin, 1997), 207–12.

What is true democracy? It is when the people, acting on their own will, have the right to choose representatives to manage affairs on the people's behalf and in accordance with the will and interests of the people. This alone can be called democracy. Furthermore, the people must have the power to replace these representatives at any time in order to keep them from abusing their powers to oppress the people. Is this actually possible? The citizens of Europe and the United States enjoy precisely this kind of democracy and can run people like Nixon, de Gaulle, and Tanaka[2] out of office when they wish and can even reinstate them if they so desire. No one can interfere with their democratic rights. In China, however, if a person even comments on the "great helmsman" or the "Great Man peerless in history," Mao Zedong, who is already dead, the mighty prison gates and all kinds of unimaginable misfortunes await him. If we compare the socialist system of "centralized democracy" with the "exploiting class democracy" of capitalism, the difference is as clear as night and day.

Will the country sink into chaos and anarchy if the people achieve democracy? On the contrary, have not the scandals exposed in the newspapers recently shown that it is precisely due to an absence of democracy that the dictators, large and small, have caused chaos and anarchy? The maintenance of democratic order is an internal problem that the people themselves must solve. It is not something that the privileged overlords need concern themselves with. Besides, they are not really concerned with democracy for the people, but use this as a pretext to deny the people of their democratic rights. Of course, internal problems cannot be solved overnight but must be constantly addressed as part of a long-term process. Mistakes and shortcomings will be inevitable, but these are for us to worry about. They are infinitely better than facing abusive overlords against whom we have no means of redress. Those who worry that democracy will lead to anarchy and chaos are just like those who, following the overthrow of the Qing dynasty,[3] worried that without an emperor, the country would fall into chaos. Their recommendation was: Patiently suffer oppression! For without the weight of oppression, the roofs of your homes might fly off!

---

[2]Richard Nixon (1913–1994), president of the United States; Charles de Gaulle (1890–1970), president of France; Kakuei Tanaka (1918–1993), prime minister of Japan.
[3]The Qing Dynasty fell in 1912 and was replaced by a republic.

To such people, I would like to say, with all due respect: We want to be the masters of our own destiny. We need no gods or emperors and we don't believe in saviors of any kind. We want to be masters of our universe; we do not want to serve as mere tools of dictators with personal ambitions for carrying out modernization. We want to modernize the lives of the people. Democracy, freedom, and happiness for all are our sole objectives in carrying out modernization. Without this "Fifth Modernization," all other modernizations are nothing but a new promise.

Comrades, I appeal to you: Let us rally together under the banner of democracy. Do not be fooled again by dictators who talk of "stability and unity." Fascist totalitarianism can bring us nothing but disaster. Harbor no more illusions; democracy is our only hope. Abandon our democratic rights and we shackle ourselves again. Let us have confidence in our own strength! We are the creators of human history. Banish all self-proclaimed leaders and teachers, for they have already cheated the people of their most valuable rights for decades.

I firmly believe that production will flourish more when controlled by the people themselves because the workers will be producing for their own benefit. Life will improve because the workers' interests will be the primary goal. Society will be more just because all power will be exercised by the people as a whole through democratic means.

I don't believe that all of this will be handed to the people effortlessly by some great savior. I also refuse to believe that China will abandon the goals of democracy, freedom, and happiness because of the many difficulties it will surely encounter along the way. As long as people clearly identify their goal and realistically assess the obstacles before them, then surely they will trample any pests that might try to bar their way.

Marching toward Modernization: Democracy in Practice

To achieve modernization, the Chinese people must first put democracy into practice and modernize China's social system. Democracy is not merely an inevitable stage of social development as Lenin claimed. In addition to being the result of productive forces and productive relations having developed to a certain stage, democracy is also the very condition that allows for the existence of such development to reach beyond this stage. Without democracy, society will become stagnant and economic growth will face insurmountable obstacles. Judging from history, therefore, a democratic social system is the premise and precondition for all development, or what we can also call modernization. Without this precondition, not only is further development impossible, but even preserving the level of development already attained would be very difficult. The experience of our great nation over the past three decades is the best evidence for this.

Why must human history follow a path toward development, or modernization? It is because humans need all of the tangible advantages that development can provide them. These advantages then enable them to achieve their foremost goal in the pursuit of happiness: freedom. Democracy is the greatest freedom ever known to man. Therefore, isn't it quite apparent why the goal of all recent human struggles has been democracy?

Why have all the reactionaries in modern history united under a common banner against democracy? It is because democracy gives their enemy—the common people—everything, and provides them—the oppressors—no weapons with which to oppose the people. The greatest reactionaries are always the greatest opponents of democracy. The histories of Germany, the Soviet Union, and "New China"[4] make this very clear and show that these reactionaries are also the most formidable and dangerous enemies of social peace and prosperity. The more recent histories of these countries make it apparent that all the struggles of the people for prosperity and of society for development are ultimately directed against the enemies of democracy—the dictatorial fascists. When democracy defeats dictatorship, it always brings with it the most favorable conditions for accelerating social development. The history of the United States offers the most convincing evidence of this.

The success of any struggle by the people for happiness, peace, and prosperity is contingent upon the quest for democracy. The success of all struggles by the people against oppression and exploitation depends upon achieving democracy. Let us throw ourselves completely into the struggle for democracy! Only through democracy can the people obtain everything. All illusions of undemocratic means are hopeless. All forms of dictatorship and totalitarianism are the most immediate and dangerous enemies of the people.

Will our enemies let us implement democracy? Of course not. They will stop at nothing to hinder the progress of democracy. Deception

---

[4]The term *New China*, which Wei uses ironically, can refer to the Communist era.

and trickery are the most effective means they have. All dictatorial fascists tell their people: Your situation is truly the best in the entire world.

Does democracy come about naturally when society reaches a certain stage? Absolutely not. A high price is paid for every tiny victory; even coming to a recognition of this fact will cost blood and sacrifice. The enemies of democracy have always deceived their people by saying that just as democracy is inevitable, it is doomed, and, therefore, it is not worth wasting energy to fight for.

But let us look at the real history, not that fabricated by the hired hacks of the "socialist government." Every small branch or twig of true and valuable democracy is stained with the blood of martyrs and tyrants, and every step taken toward democracy has been fiercely attacked by the reactionary forces. The fact that democracy has been able to surmount such obstacles proves that it is precious to the people and that it embodies their aspirations. Therefore the democratic trend cannot be stopped. The Chinese people have never feared anything. They need only recognize the direction to be taken and the forces of tyranny will no longer be invincible.

Is the struggle for democracy what the Chinese people want? The Cultural Revolution was the first time they flexed their muscles, and all the reactionary forces trembled before them. But at that time the people had no clear direction and the force of democracy was not the main thrust of their struggle. As a result, the dictators silenced most of them through bribes, deception, division, slander, or violent suppression. At the time, people also had a blind faith in all kinds of ambitious dictators, so once again they unwittingly became the tools and sacrificial lambs of tyrants and potential tyrants.

Now, twelve years later, the people have finally recognized their goal. They see clearly the real direction of their fight and have found their true leader: the banner of democracy. The Democracy Wall at Xidan has become the first battlefield in the people's fight against the reactionary forces. The struggle will be victorious—this is already a commonly accepted belief; the people will be liberated—this slogan has already taken on new significance. There may be bloodshed and sacrifice, and people may fall prey to even more sinister plots, yet the banner of democracy will never again be obscured by the evil fog of the reactionary forces. Let us unite together under this great and true banner and march toward modernization of society for the sake of the tranquillity, happiness, rights, and freedom of all the people!

3

DESMOND TUTU

Change or Illusion?

March 1980

Bishop Desmond Tutu (1931–) of the Anglican Church delivered this speech to the Black Sash, an organization of white women in South Africa that promoted nonviolent resistance to apartheid. The apartheid system sought to segregate South Africa's racial communities from one another and thus to maintain white supremacy. Tutu won the Nobel Peace Prize in 1984 for his efforts to end this brutal discrimination and to heal the sharp divisions in South Africa. After the fall of apartheid in 1994, he gained new renown as the head of the Truth and Reconciliation Commission, which examined the crimes of that regime. Two events would have been much in the minds of his audience in 1980: the Soweto Uprising in 1976, which had left hundreds dead, many of them school-children; and the end of white rule in Rhodesia (now Zimbabwe) earlier in 1980. Bishop Tutu, in turn, is concerned with how even the most liberal-minded whites, who enjoyed freedom and prosperity comparable to Western Europeans, must examine their complicity in repression.

There are those of us in South Africa who will go into ecstasies about the changes that have happened. Is the government not removing all discriminatory signs; don't we have multi-racial sport? People can now go to so-called international hotels and restaurants (never mind the embarrassments when you don't know which of these facilities are available for all races or not) and the Prime Minister has himself with considerable courage, veritably bearding the lion in his den, made those pronouncements about adapting or dying and about improving the Immorality and Mixed Marriages Acts (whatever improving might be construed to mean). All these and similar facts surely point to change happening in South Africa? . . . They do not affect the structures of the unjust apartheid society in any significant way at all. . . .

From Desmond Tutu, "Change or Illusion?" March 1980, University of Cape Town Library, Manuscripts and Archives Division.

I suppose the divided state of our nation is showed up nowhere more dramatically than in the whole area of defense and so-called patriotism. . . . Most whites, especially Afrikaners but not only they, are cock-a-hoop about defense. They believe they are defending South Africa against the onslaught of communism. Many blacks are quite sure they find very little to defend about present day South Africa. I am totally opposed to communism and marxism. . . . I would be willing to defend South Africa against communism but that is not my priority concern. Communism is a potential enemy. My priority concern is the present state of injustice and oppression of which I and fellow blacks are victims in the land of our birth. There is nothing potential about that: it is a brutal actuality and that is what most blacks want to defend themselves against here and now.

. . . I believe that the polarization I have been describing is a very serious matter and that it seems to be getting worse by the day. . . . We are reaping the whirlwind due to the success of apartheid. . . .

"What can we do?" That is almost always the cry from many whites when they are faced with the stark realities of our situation and they are sincere people who do want to change things. I know there are others who want change as long as things remain much the same, as long as their privileges are not lost, as long as their high standard of living remains unaffected. There always tends to be some sense of impotence because they are faced with what seems to be a colossus. I am very sympathetic with my white fellow South Africans but I have no real sympathy with what I believe is an imagined impotence. You do after all have the power of the ballot box. When the Indians in India were incensed with Mrs. Indira Gandhi, they got rid of her.[1] When the British were browned off with the conservatives not even a Winston Churchill could save them from a devastating postwar defeat at the polls.[2] . . . So if South African whites really mean business then they have the remedy in their own hands. . . .

Do you recall a strange case a few years ago when we had a colossal butter surplus? By some convoluted economics the dairy board decided that since there was a surplus the price of butter should go up. I used to think that the free enterprise system decreed that if there is oversupply then the price has to go down to increase demand.

---

[1]*Indira Gandhi* (1917–1984): prime minister of India from 1966 to 1977, when her party lost an election. She returned to power in 1980 and was assassinated in 1984.

[2]In July 1945, just two months after the end of World War II, Prime Minister Winston Churchill's Conservative party was defeated by the Labour party.

Never mind—I'm no economist. What I want to remind you is that women decided they were not going to buy butter until sanity was restored. For a while they succeeded in getting the price of butter reduced. . . . The government does often take note when strong feelings are aroused about this or that. . . .

Another point to be made is this: don't look for spectacular achievements. Do what you can in your little corner: "bietjie bietjie maak meer" [Afrikaans: Drop by drop one makes a sea]. You know, don't you, that the sea is only single drops of water collected together. If there were no single drops of water there would be no sea. . . .

To the government I want to say what I have said times without number: nobody expects all the changes to happen overnight. Rome we are told was not built in one day. Politics is the art of the possible. You don't want to alienate your supporters and so erode your power-base. We are prepared to exercise some patience provided you demonstrate your commitment to real change.

First of all, say clearly and unequivocally that you are committed to an undivided non-racial South Africa. That for us blacks is quite unnegotiable: our citizenship in an undivided South Africa. If we get this commitment we are ready to tell our people to hold their horses because these chaps are now talking business.

At present no one in government has repudiated Dr. Mulder's statement (quite breathtaking) that the logical goal of apartheid is that there will be no black South Africans.[3] If that be the case, then I want to issue a warning as responsibly and as dispassionately as possible. It is this: if South Africa is to be balkanized and blacks stripped of their South African citizenship, then you can kiss goodbye to any chances of a peaceful solution. . . . God is good to us: he says "I want to give you an object lesson on how not to solve a political crisis," and he has provided us with Rhodesia.[4] Let's not say it can't happen to us, it always happens to the other guy. . . .

---

[3]Cornelius Mulder, a minister in the South African government, made this statement in a speech to Parliament in February 1978. Mulder was defending the "Bantustan" or "homeland" policy, in which the government created territories for different African ethnicities and forced black South Africans to take "citizenship" in these lands. No other country ever recognized these territories, and residents in them remained wholly dependent on the South African economy.

[4]White leaders of the British colony of Rhodesia, including Prime Minister Ian Smith, attempted to retain control in the face of international pressure; they were defeated in 1979 by an insurgency led by Robert Mugabe. Rhodesia gained its independence as Zimbabwe in April 1980.

All the current black political leaders who are acknowledged as such by the black community are ready to talk. It is no use engaging in what appears to be a charade with leaders whom most blacks repudiate. . . . Our real leaders are eminently reasonable men and I include those on Robben Island[5] and those in exile. Percy Qoboza[6] pointed out that these were the last generation that will be ready to negotiate. Please let us talk whilst we can, whilst there is the real possibility of an orderly evolution to a shared society. I have dedicated myself to help bring this about and yet when you hear some references to people such as . . . myself, you could be forgiven for thinking that we were fire-spouting radical marxists who were toting Russian made guns.

To the white community in general I say: express your commitment to change by agreeing to accept a redistribution of wealth and a more equitable sharing of the resources of our land. Be willing to accept voluntarily a declension in your very high standard of living. Isn't it better to have lost something voluntarily and to assist in bringing about change—political powersharing—in an orderly fashion than to see this change come with bloodshed and chaos when you stand to lose everything. Change your attitudes. Know that blacks are human beings and all we want is to be treated as such. Everything you want for yourselves is exactly what we want for ourselves and for our children: a stable family life where the husband lives with his wife and children, adequate housing and proper free and compulsory education for our children and all the social services you take for granted— electrification, paved streets, parks, lighted streets, swimming pools, and don't say you have earned them and pay for them because we are victims of a cheap labor system and are quite willing to pay for these things if we are paid the rate for the job. . . .

All of these items . . . comprise what could be the harbingers of change. I want to add just one more: the possibility of free discussion of various options politically, religiously, economically and socially. We are inhibited in our land from canvassing various possibilities. Let us hear about Marxism and communism. If democracy is superior to them as I believe it is, then they stand no chance of being tempting. Part of their attraction lies in that they are forbidden fruit. Let us discuss alternatives to a violent solution and so let's talk about sanctions openly and responsibly. You know my experience after Denmark.[7] I have never

---

[5]*Robben Island*: the prison for leading black opponents of the apartheid regime.
[6]*Percy Qoboza*: a leading South African journalist who died in 1988.
[7]In an interview on Danish television in late 1979, Tutu called it "rather disgraceful" that Denmark bought coal from South Africa.

been so vilified and become the object of so much white hostility and vituperation (I have also been comforted by the support of many). You could have thought that I had said in Denmark "now blacks let's go on the rampage and rape white women" and not that I was looking for peaceful and nonviolent methods for helping to persuade those with power to come to the negotiating table before it was disastrously late, and to point out my own anguish and anger at the suffering deliberately inflicted on our people in the resettlement camps.

. . . Yes let there be more open and free discussions. I believe we still have a chance if we grab the opportunity God has given us. I am still committed to reasonably peaceful change and I am committed to work for justice and reconciliation. But the sands of time are running out quickly. Let's do something to avert the bloodbath; the alternative is too ghastly to contemplate. . . . Will somebody take heed, please.

4

MEHDI BAZARGAN

Religion and Liberty

1983

One region of the world that saw no democratic revolutions in the late cold war period is the Middle East. Indeed, the era is marked by the violent Iranian Revolution of 1979 and by the first Palestinian intifada, *or rebellion, which began in 1987. The reasons for this failure are beyond the scope of this book. Yet the region was not without proponents of tolerance and of freedom of expression.*

Mehdi Bazargan (1907–1995) was a prominent supporter of the Iranian Revolution and the Islamic Republic's first prime minister. He and his government resigned in November 1979 after the storming of the U.S. embassy and the taking of hostages there. Bazargan remained a member of parliament but continued to protest the revolution's move toward harsh repression, as well as the dominance in Iranian politics of

From Mehdi Bazargan, "Religion and Liberty," in *Liberal Islam: A Sourcebook*, ed. Charles Kurzman (New York: Oxford University Press, 1998), 81–84.

religious leaders like the Ayatollah Khomeini. In this essay, he rejects "religious tyranny," asserting that God is a better judge of what is right for humans than are people themselves. He then argues, in the excerpt that follows, that freedom is in fact necessary and does not at all contradict faith. His argument reveals his scientific training: He received a doctorate in thermodynamics at the University of Paris.

Let me reiterate: freedom means freedom to oppose, criticize, and object—even if the criticism is untrue and unjust. Where there is freedom there are opponents and currents that disturb routine stability and normalcy. Otherwise, freedom would be meaningless and useless.

This notion of freedom is hard for many zealous—if sincere—people to digest, as they consider such a freedom unwise and deleterious to the survival of the nascent Islamic Republic [of Iran]. They may even consider it a blunder on their part to have allowed this notion of freedom to prevail in the constitution of the Islamic Republic of Iran.

However, omniscient, compassionate God has not only sanctioned freedom in many affairs, he has made it the very foundation of survival and revival in the world. Let me elaborate on this point.

Opposition, the Cause of Movement and Life

In general, an object in a given force field will, of necessity, behave in a calculable and predictable way. For any object, whether a stone, a plant, or a human society, force means movement. For example, a piece of metal that is released within earth's gravitational field will fall in a straight line. Its position and velocity are calculable at every moment. Similarly, the behavior of a human being who is motivated only by the demands of his or her appetite is predictable. However, if in the place of one force, two or more forces are introduced—for example if a powerful magnet is placed in the path of the falling piece of metal—its trajectory and velocity will change. It will, to use a poetic expression, be freed from the slavery of a single cause of motion. The scenario is most intriguing when the affected object has the power to choose its level of susceptibility to the external influences. That is, when it has "free will." In this case, the person whose choice is not readily predictable and calculable for others—or even for oneself—could be said to possess "free will."

Therefore, freedom requires, as the case of Satan's temptations teach us, the existence of an oppositional force, along with a power of choice on behalf of the individual or the society. Opposition promulgates movement and change, which may, in turn, lead to decline or progress, depending on the choice of the agent involved.

Motion and change in the case of inanimate objects, even constructed objects such as machines, lead to erosion and deterioration (in the jargon of thermodynamic theory, the increase of entropy). In other words, inanimate objects aim at final rest and quiet. However, objects endowed with life, particularly human beings, thrive on movement and opposition. They acquire new capabilities and aptitudes and accumulate experience and virtue because of opposition and change. Movement, a result of need, agitation, and love, is a blessing and a source of survival and evolution, while rigidity is a cause of stasis, decline, and death. Animals and human beings, once they feel need, danger, or attraction, tend to move, willy-nilly, either toward the object of their desire or away from the source of danger. Therefore, without opposition as a source of motivation or agitation there would be no progress. The oppositional motivator can lead to reform and revival.

Our Islamic Revolution, our nationalist struggles, revivalist Islamic associations and movements, the earlier Constitutional Revolution of Iran—the awakening and activism of the Eastern countries in general after several hundred years of slumber and humiliation—were all the result of the encounter with Western civilization. The wondrous European Renaissance too was a result of conflicts, dissatisfactions, and objection to medieval Christian hegemony.

Similarly, the missions of the prophets were in the past the source of conflicts that revolutionized towns and tribes that were wallowing in the darkness of idolatry and the cesspool of corruption and inequity.

Conflict, one of whose quintessential representations for human beings is Satan, is the cause of a plethora of blessed events, from the natural cycle of life here on earth to the higher cycle of resurrection in the hereafter. The Qur'an [Koran] frequently compares the colossal events of Judgment Day with seasonal rain and the revival of life on earth. Rain itself is the result of atmospheric disturbances and opposing forces of cold and warm weather systems. The science of meteorology has established, through hourly reports from weather stations, that rain-bearing continental weather fronts are comprised of successive fronts of dense clouds. These clouds are the results of expanding, rising, and condensing warm tropical weather and its collision with the cold and heavy weather systems that flow from the northern regions. The heavy winds occupy the lower areas and push the warm humid weather up.

The Opponents of Freedom

The opponents of freedom resort to the adage: "A head that does not ache does not need to be wrapped." Their argument goes like this: We know we are on the true path. We believe in Islam and possess good will and proper judgment. What need is there for further inquiry and learning? We can simply devote ourselves, body and soul, to the realization of the true doctrine. The entire nation and its leadership support this endeavor. Why should we let the enemies of God and the republic, the supporters of America, or those who do not follow our line—in short, people of suspicious intent or judgment—to muddy the waters, confuse minds, disturb society, and weaken the government? Such freedom and criticism will provide fodder for foreign radio propaganda which will, in turn, cause our youth to hesitate or deviate from the straight path. It is thus better to remove all the impediments from the path of the revolution and to conduct our affairs quickly and effectively—that is, without the nagging distractions of free expression and opposition.

These gentlemen, even if they are sincere, are deluded and naive about their own monopoly of the truth and about the notion of freedom. Freedom is not a luxury; it is a necessity. When freedom is banished, tyranny will take its place. . . .

Secondly, freedom of expression, opposition, and criticism awakens the negligent and holds back treason, monopoly, and tyranny. If the objections are unjustified, let the accused respond and thus dispel the clouds of suspicion and slander. This will strengthen the national resolve. The Qur'an considers such examinations as the means of separating the good from the bad. Conversely, suppression of freedom is an indication of a fundamental weakness or flaw in the government's intentions or actions. . . .

Thus the survival of a just system and its progress on the path of virtue and excellence is guaranteed by the freedom of expression and legal opposition. The protection of religion against abuse, ignorance, superstition, and deviance, too, requires that the mace of excommunication and compulsion be removed from society and the media. It is necessary to avoid painting a varnish of religiosity and godliness on human affairs, save that which necessarily and authentically belongs to religion. It is also necessary that some room is left for reflection and maneuver in all debates.

. . . God addresses people themselves immediately and directly, without intermediaries. Everyone is directly responsible, and people's reason, knowledge, thought, perception, reflection, and will are the ultimate arbiter. We have the Qur'anic injunction, "If you do not know, then ask the keepers of (knowledge and) remembrance" (Sura[1] 21, Verse 7), which indicates that it is proper to inquire, and to augment one's knowledge. In the meantime, the Qur'an has envisioned, without censure, the existence and expression of disagreements and differences of opinion among the faithful. It recommends the disagreements with the rulers to be referred to the Prophet and to God, which in our days would mean the body of religious knowledge.

Disagreement becomes unacceptable and disruptive only when it takes place at the executive level and when the responsible managers, instead of harmony and disciplined cooperation, engage in discord and in-fighting, each playing their own tune and doing their own thing. The principle of division of powers and their mutual non-interference and orderly checks and balances pervades Iran's old and new constitutions, and those of other parliamentary democratic systems. People and their representatives have a right to discuss, investigate, supervise, and decide public affairs within certain limits and without interfering in the progress, rigor, and effective management of the executive affairs as determined by the legislature. And now let me address the questions that were posed earlier:

Has Islam abandoned people to do whatever they please? Is there no responsibility and restraint in this world?

Being free and autonomous is one thing, and being responsible for one's beliefs and actions quite another. God has given us freedom of opinion and action within certain parameters, but He has given us plenty of warning through His messengers and holy books, that rebellion, disbelief, and injustice will have dire results that will follow from our actions both in this life and in the hereafter. . . .

God bestows both freedom and guidance concerning the consequences of actions. His mercy is infinite and His vengeance great. Thus freedom exists; so do responsibility and restraint. The choice is ours. . . .

Should the Islamic government and the religious scholars in the leadership not check crime and treason? Should chaos and license rule?

The issue of individual liberty in violation of others' rights has been addressed in the first question. Absolute freedom of choice, as we understand it in the Qur'an, prevails in the relationship of God and man—not in that of society and the individual, where mutual rights

---

[1] *Sura*: chapter of the Qur'an.

and responsibilities are at stake. God may forgive transgression against His laws but, as we know, God cannot forgive people for transgressing against the rights of people. We do not enjoy the same level of freedom in our dealings with other people as we do in our personal relationship with God.

5

JULIETA KIRKWOOD

Feminism's Time

1983

Democracy activists like those who appear in this book tend to feel that they are striving for the liberation of all people and for human and civil rights for everyone in their country. Therefore, they often argue, the rights of women and other groups would naturally be achieved as a by-product of freedom. Sometimes this reasoning was explicit, but most of the time it was subconscious. Female activists generally accepted this perspective; strong, public feminist movements were rare in undemocratic countries in the 1980s. Chile is a significant exception, thanks in part to the work of Julieta Kirkwood (1936–1985). A sociologist by training, Kirkwood co-organized a number of social movements and independent research groups focused on women's issues. At first, she studied the living and working experiences of poor Chilean women. She then began to focus on feminist theory and its relationship to the struggle against dictator Augusto Pinochet. It may seem strange that, in the following essay, Kirkwood directs more scorn at fellow socialists, captured in a belated moment of discovery, than at the enemy regime. However, she takes the common enemy as a given and shows how feminism and the position of women are central to the struggle for democracy, as in the phrase that became the most-recognized slogan of the Chilean women's movement: "Democracy in the country and in the home."

From Julieta Kirkwood, "Tiempo de feminismo," *Tejiendo Rebeldías: Escritos Feministas de Julieta Kirkwood,* ed. Patricia Crispi (Santiago: Centro de Estudios de la Mujer and Casa de la Mujer La Morada, 1987), 44–46. Translated by José Najar.

Until very recently, the topic of feminism and women's liberation was notably absent from the great debates, plenary sessions, and seminars conducted by the Chilean left, both at home and in exile. At most, it was mentioned in paragraph number seven or so; at most there was a grateful tribute to the support of noble female comrades in the struggle; at most, vague references to the important role in social change that certain feminine organizations with a "clear view of history" had played in the past or might someday play.

Many of these women's organizations themselves very often hushed up and postponed their specific demands in the spirit of the axiom "There is no feminism without democracy." This phrase is simply another way of reaffirming the sequence: "Fight first against the dictatorship and for democracy; the woman problem, later."

This logic of "later," so precise and fair, does not exactly come up in this way in real life; it is a feeling experienced intensely by feminist groups here and over there.[1] Nevertheless, this feeling that women's issues are being suppressed can today be greatly lessened in concrete Chilean political practice. A seminar on "Chile in the Eighties," organized by the Socialist Convergence in June of this year, gave us a compelling example.

About 300 people from various groups, political parties, or social movements spoke at the seminar and gave their opinion about a democratic and socialist alternative for Chile.[2] Many of them were women, many of them feminists, and all very active. To the discussion of traditional topics, like trade unions, youth, economics, politics, and international relations, the seminar added the unveiling of a "mixed" political debate about "Women's Liberation."

Here's how it went, in all its glory:

First, there was a moment of amazement, surprise, and expectation. Nervous giggles, semi-joking whistling, winks and elbows accompanied by masculine whispers soon gave way to strong support for a Commission to discuss "Women."

We believe that this curiosity was in part a response to boredom with what had already been discussed, with the common knowledge of

---

[1] "Over there" refers to the Chilean opposition in exile.

[2] Kirkwood would have drawn a clear distinction between her socialism, a program of democracy and social justice, and the top-down, state-driven forms in the Soviet Union and China. The terminology can be confusing; what Mikhail Gorbachev (Document 7) or Yuan Mu (Document 30) called "socialism" most outside observers called "communism."

more conventional issues; maybe the promise of political renewal contained in the public announcement of the seminar, perhaps the promise of something not yet defined, not yet transformed into a party line. . . . In the end, they needed to form two groups to accommodate nearly eighty interested men and women.

And only then . . . the debate began! And sex mixed with politics; we discussed how societies are restricted and badly organized. And the voices were shy or joyful, sometimes painful, always contagious; the feminist voices spoke of personal experiences, of excluding worlds, of the "feminine" and the "masculine," of the corrupting bias of socialization. There was discussion of patriarchal history, of the impact of its features on the genesis of authoritarian rule, of the system of discipline; of the denial of affection for some, and the denial of rationality to others, of the doubt, the great doubt in Order;[3] of the intimate feeling of being a person. Protests new and old were voiced against a society punished and violated by the strict codes that deny pleasure and liberty.

And there, between words and silences, that very subtle and elusive link between the material-economic, the socio-political, and individual dignity was achieved.

And we forgot to discuss the general document.[4]

The voices of this and that group became blurred, joining together as one, and triggered an understanding of roads not traveled. The "Wait for Later" no longer made sense to anyone. A new concept for changing socialist life rooted itself—this concept of what is political in everyday life, in the HERE AND NOW, in what is palpable, in the way of relating to each other.

In sum, at last there was a glimpse of light on something new: the freshness of talking without codes, or, even better, of transgressing them. The novelty of recovering women's and men's experiences and seeing the urgent relationship between feminism and global liberation. An attempt to rid oneself of worn concepts, of those problems which are assumed to be "serious," with serious attributes. An attempt to dilate the meaning of things until they explode, giving birth to their sundry contents. To reveal the future they hold. To cut through any doubts but always raising one more, with the only requirement to fully open one's eyes and mind.

---

[3]Kirkwood's readers would connect "Order" with the regime of Augusto Pinochet, who promised to restore order to Chile; his supporters viewed the brief rule of President Salvador Allende (1970–1973) as a descent into anarchy. See Chapter 4.

[4]Probably, as would be typical at a party conference, the meeting on women's issues was supposed to discuss a prepared text.

Later on, one could overhear a man surprised by the clarity of what the women said, by their well-founded judgments, by their serious, reasoned yet emotional commitment [to the cause], by their reflectiveness.

Some, perhaps the minority, imagined that they would stoically receive the complaints, laments, and grievances against the traditional machismo of both the elite and the common person. And they prepared their well-knit, armored, slippery arguments: "Yes, but at home I . . ."

Well, whatever. They realized that it was about changing life, not adding small patches or changes of color, not about hanging some more women's names in the offices, in political commissions, or in occupational statistics. They realized that it was more than just "helping out at home." They found themselves in front of knowledgeable women, and then they understood, because now they know the magnitude of what has been lost to mankind when the submission and submissiveness of half of humanity have been accepted, for a long time, for many thousands of years. So much destruction, death, fighting, persecution, and perversion in the cause of maintaining inequalities within the intimacies of the family.

Regarding that "Wait for Later," we found ourselves at a point where there is no reasonable doubt that neither democracy, nor even less socialism, will be constructed—they cannot be built—if we push aside and defer the "women problem." We find that it is necessary and possible to acknowledge this problem, to see it, to assume it, even amidst the most outrageous denial of democracy, NOW, in order for the liberation of human society to be thinkable, imaginable. . . . And this is not difficult: it is achieved simply by looking at our own daily actions. Men rely upon the work performed by others—women— who tirelessly organize and plan all the concrete aspects of daily life by means of "small household chores," which are not valued, are not valuable; which are stuck in the "private" sphere, the sphere that signifies "that which is deprived" . . . the essence of deprivation.

That weekend, part of the domestic curtain was drawn aside, with political courtesy, to show the constraints, injustices, and inequalities that are stored there, shaped, and scrupulously constrained in the name of love, of maternity, of social order, of the necessity to first do what has always been that way.

But what has been seen through socialist eyes cannot be dissipated with a new beat of the eyelids of necessity. The complex socialist road is more than just the path of State. It is the road where life is changed. When we ask for democracy in the country and in the home, we simply mean that socialism can begin, and can be achieved, at home.

6

AUNG SAN SUU KYI

In Quest of Democracy

1988

The daughter of Burma's founder, Aung San (assassinated in 1947), Aung San Suu Kyi (1945–) spent much of her adult life in Britain until she returned home in 1988. Burma (today called Myanmar) was then, as it remains in the present day, in the grip of a military regime espousing an idiosyncratic form of authoritarian socialism. Student-led unrest that year exploded into mass demonstrations on August 8; the uprising was crushed with much loss of life. Aung San Suu Kyi remained in Burma and became both an iconic figure and the leading proponent of human rights and democratic change. She was then detained and placed under house arrest in July 1989, where she has remained (with brief interludes) ever since.

In May 1990, Suu Kyi's National League for Democracy won a parliamentary election, making her the legitimate political leader of Burma. She was awarded the Nobel Peace Prize in 1991. In this document, Suu Kyi argues that democracy is not foreign to Burmese traditions or values, including Buddhist beliefs, and shows how those beliefs and values could guide the Burmese to resist dictatorship.

The people of Burma view democracy not merely as a form of government but as an integrated social and ideological system based on respect for the individual. When asked why they feel so strong a need for democracy, the least political will answer: "We just want to be able to go about our own business freely and peacefully, not doing anybody any harm, just earning a decent living without anxiety and fear." In other words they want the basic human rights which would guarantee a tranquil, dignified existence free from want and fear. "Democracy songs" articulated such longings: "I am not among the rice-eating robots.... Everyone but everyone should be entitled to human rights." "We are

From Aung San Suu Kyi, "In Quest of Democracy," in Aung San Suu Kyi, *Freedom from Fear and Other Writings*, ed. Michael Aris (New York: Viking, 1991), 173–78.

not savage beasts of the jungle, we are all men with reason, it's high time to stop the rule of armed intimidation: if every movement of dissent were settled by the gun, Burma would only be emptied of people."

It was predictable that as soon as the issue of human rights became an integral part of the movement for democracy the official media should start ridiculing and condemning the whole concept of human rights, dubbing it a western artifact alien to traditional values. It was also ironic—Buddhism, the foundation of traditional Burmese culture, places the greatest value on man, who alone of all beings can achieve the supreme state of Buddhahood. Each man has in him the potential to realize the truth through his own will and endeavor and to help others to realize it. Human life therefore is infinitely precious. "Easier is it for a needle dropped from the abode of Brahma¹ to meet a needle stuck in the earth than to be born as a human being."

But despotic governments do not recognize the precious human component of the state, seeing its citizens only as a faceless, mindless—and helpless—mass to be manipulated at will. It is as though people were incidental to a nation rather than its very lifeblood. Patriotism, which should be the vital love and care of a people for their land, is debased into a smokescreen of hysteria to hide the injustices of authoritarian rulers who define the interests of the state in terms of their own limited interests. The official creed is required to be accepted with an unquestioning faith more in keeping with orthodox tenets of the biblical religions which have held sway in the West than with the more liberal Buddhist attitude:

> It is proper to doubt, to be uncertain. . . . Do not go upon what has been acquired by repeated hearing. Nor upon tradition, nor upon rumors. . . . When you know for yourself that certain things are unwholesome and wrong, abandon them. . . . When you know for yourself that certain things are wholesome and good, accept them.

It is a puzzlement to the Burmese how concepts which recognize the inherent dignity and the equal and inalienable rights of human beings, which accept that all men are endowed with reason and conscience and which recommend a universal spirit of brotherhood, can be inimical to indigenous values. It is also difficult for them to understand how any of the rights contained in the thirty articles of the Universal Declaration of Human Rights² can be seen as anything but

---

¹*Brahma*: the Hindu god of creation, traditionally believed to reside on a very high mountain.

²The United Nations adopted the Universal Declaration of Human Rights on December 10, 1948. This date is commemorated worldwide as Human Rights Day.

wholesome and good. That the declaration was not drawn up in Burma by the Burmese seems an inadequate reason, to say the least, for rejecting it, especially as Burma was one of the nations which voted for its adoption in December 1948. If ideas and beliefs are to be denied validity outside the geographical and cultural bounds of their origin, Buddhism would be confined to north India, Christianity to a narrow tract in the Middle East and Islam to Arabia.

The proposition that the Burmese are not fit to enjoy as many rights and privileges as the citizens of democratic countries is insulting. It also makes questionable the logic of a Burmese government considering itself fit to enjoy more rights and privileges than the governments of those same countries. The inconsistency can be explained—but not justified—only by assuming so wide a gulf between the government and the people that they have to be judged by different norms. Such an assumption in turn casts doubt on the doctrine of government as a comprehensive spirit and medium of national values.

Weak logic, inconsistencies and alienation from the people are common features of authoritarianism. The relentless attempts of totalitarian regimes to prevent free thought and new ideas and the persistent assertion of their own rightness bring on them an intellectual stasis which they project on to the nation at large. Intimidation and propaganda work in a duet of oppression, while the people, lapped in fear and distrust, learn to dissemble and to keep silent. And all the time the desire grows for a system which will lift them from the position of "rice-eating robots" to the status of human beings who can think and speak freely and hold their heads high in the security of their rights.

From the beginning Burma's struggle for democracy has been fraught with danger. A movement which seeks the just and equitable distribution of powers and prerogatives that have long been held by a small elite determined to preserve its privileges at all costs is likely to be prolonged and difficult. Hope and optimism are irrepressible but there is a deep underlying premonition that the opposition to change is likely to be vicious. Often the anxious question is asked: will such an oppressive regime *really* give us democracy? And the answer has to be: democracy, like liberty, justice and other social and political rights, is not "given," it is earned through courage, resolution and sacrifice.

Revolutions generally reflect the irresistible impulse for necessary changes which have been held back by official policies or retarded by social apathy. The institutions and practices of democracy provide ways and means by which such changes could be effected without recourse to violence. But change is anathema to authoritarianism, which will tolerate no deviation from rigid policies. Democracy acknowledges the right to differ as well as the duty to settle differences peacefully. Authoritarian governments see criticism of their actions and doctrines as a challenge to combat. Opposition is equaled with "confrontation," which is interpreted as violent conflict. Regimented minds cannot grasp the concept of confrontation as an open exchange of major differences with a view to settlement through genuine dialogue. The insecurity of power based on coercion translates into a need to crush all dissent. Within the framework of liberal democracy, protest and dissent can exist in healthy counterpart with orthodoxy and conservatism, contained by a general recognition of the need to balance respect for individual rights with respect for law and order.

The words "law and order" have so frequently been misused as an excuse for oppression that the very phrase has become suspect in countries which have known authoritarian rule. Some years ago a prominent Burmese author wrote an article on the notion of law and order as expressed by the official term *nyein-wul-pi-pyar*. One by one he analyzed the words, which literally mean "quiet-crouched-crushed-flattened," and concluded that the whole made for an undesirable state of affairs, one which militated against the qualities that the people of Burma are seeing in their struggle for democracy.

In a revolutionary movement there is always the danger that political exigencies might obscure, or even nullify, essential spiritual aims. A firm insistence on the inviolability and primacy of such aims is not mere idealism but a necessary safeguard against an Animal Farm[3] syndrome where the new order after its first flush of enthusiastic reforms takes on the murky colors of the very system it has replaced. The people of Burma want not just a change of government but a change in political values. The unhappy legacies of authoritarianism can be removed only if the concept of absolute power as the basis of government is replaced by the concept of confidence of the people in their right and ability to decide the destiny of their nation, the mutual confidence in the principles of justice, liberty and human rights. Of the four Buddhist virtues conducive to the happiness of laymen, *saddha*, confidence in moral, spiritual and intellectual values, is the first. To instill such confidence, not by an appeal to the passions but through intellectual conviction, into a society which has long been wracked by distrust and uncertainty is the essence of the Burmese revolution for democracy. It is a revolution which moves for changes endorsed by universal norms of ethics.

---

[3] *Animal Farm*: a dystopian novel by George Orwell (1945).

In the quest for democracy the people of Burma explore not only the political theories and practices of the world outside their country but also the spiritual and intellectual values that have given shape to their own environment.

7

MIKHAIL GORBACHEV

On Socialist Democracy

January 1987

When Mikhail Gorbachev (1931–) was chosen to be general secretary of the Communist party of the Soviet Union in March 1985, he was only fifty-four years old. His relative youth contributed to his awareness that the Soviet Union needed swift reform if it were to survive. The Soviet economy was in disastrous shape, hampered particularly by the deeply entrenched bureaucracy's resistance to change.

Gorbachev's speech to a plenary meeting of the Central Committee in January 1987 can be considered the most important political speech in the USSR since a previous general secretary, Nikita Khrushchev (1894–1971), addressed the crimes of Stalinism in a secret speech in February 1956. In this speech, Gorbachev uses the terms perestroika *(restructuring) and* glasnost *(openness), which became internationally recognized as the basis for Soviet economic and political change. Although Gorbachev failed to save the regime, he did signal to the world that the days of highly centralized control were over. This contributed to the movements for change in Eastern Europe as well as in the Soviet Union.*

Elements of social corrosion that emerged in recent years have adversely affected society's morale and insidiously eroded the high moral values which have always been characteristic of our people and of which we are proud, namely, ideological conviction, labor enthusiasm and Soviet patriotism. . . .

From Mikhail S. Gorbachev, "On Socialist Democracy," in Mikhail Gorbachev, *Socialism, Peace and Democracy: Writings, Speeches and Reports* (Atlantic Highlands, N.J.: Zwan, 1987), 114–15, 118–19, 121, 129–30, 133–36, 138, 160, 162.

Disregard for laws, report-padding, bribe-taking and encouragement of toadyism and adulation had a deleterious effect on the moral
atmosphere in society. Real care for people, for the conditions of
their life and work and for their social well-being was often sup-
planted by political flirtation—the mass distribution of awards, titles
and prizes. . . .
    The world of day-to-day realities and that of make-believe well-
being were increasingly parting ways. . . .
    In this situation, comrades, the question of accelerating the socio-
economic development of the country, the question of *perestroika* was
raised. . . .
    We must make this decisive turn because there is no other choice.
We must not retreat and there is no place to retreat to. . . .
    Today it is essential to say once again what we mean by *perestroika*.
Perestroika is a resolute overcoming of the processes of stagnation,
destruction of the retarding mechanism, and the creation of depend-
able and efficient machinery for expediting the social and economic
progress of Soviet society. . . .
    Perestroika is reliance on the creative endeavor of the masses, an
all-round extension of democracy and socialist self-government, the
encouragement of initiative and self-organized activities, better discipline and order, greater openness, criticism and self-criticism in all
fields of public life, and full and proper respect for the value and dignity of the individual. . . .
    It is only through the consistent development of the democratic
forms inherent in socialism and more extensive self-government that
our progress in production, science and technology, literature, culture
and the arts, in all areas of social life is possible. It is only this way
that ensures conscientious discipline. *Perestroika* itself is possible only
through democracy and because of democracy. It is only this way that
it is possible to open broad vistas for socialism's most powerful creative force—free labor and free thought in a free country. . . .
    What ways does the Political Bureau see to further deepen democ-
racy in Soviet society? . . .
    Of paramount importance is the development of democracy in pro-
duction and the consistent implementation of the principles of working
people's self-management. . . . This is the lever that will enable us to
ensure the broad and active participation of the working people in all
areas of social life and make it possible to avoid many errors and
miscalculations. . . .
    From the political point of view it is a question of enhancing the
democratic nature of the electoral system and of a more effective and

real involvement of the electorate at all stages of the pre-election and election campaigns.

Concretely, most proposals [sent to Party authorities] suggest that voters at meetings in work collectives and at places of residence, as well as at election meetings, discuss . . . several candidacies, that elections be held in larger constituencies, and that several deputies be elected from each of them. People believe that this would enable each citizen to express his attitude to a greater number of candidates and would enable Party and local government bodies to get to know better the sentiments and will of the population.

. . . It is essential to rid the voting procedure of formalism and to see to it that the election campaign of even this year be held in an atmosphere of broader democracy with the interested participation of the people. . . .

But with all the importance of control "from above" it is of fundamental importance in the conditions of the democratization of society to raise the level and effectiveness of control "from below" so that each executive and each official constantly feels his responsibility to and dependence on the electorate, on the work collectives, public organizations, on the Party and the people as a whole. The main thing in this respect is to create and strengthen all instruments and forms of real control by the working people.

What instruments do I have in mind?

Accountability, first of all. The time has come to observe strictly the rules for systematic accountability of all elected and appointed officials before work collectives and the population. It is necessary that every such account be accompanied by lively and principled discussion, criticism and self-criticism and businesslike proposals, and end with an evaluation of the activities of the person giving an account of his work.

. . . In the conditions of extended democracy people themselves will put things in order in their work collective, town or village. . . .

While normalizing the atmosphere in society it is essential to further encourage *glasnost*. This is a powerful lever for improving work in all sectors of our development and an effective form of control by the whole people. . . .

Obviously the time has come to begin elaborating legal acts guaranteeing *glasnost*. These should ensure maximum *glasnost* in the activities of state and public organizations and give the working people a real opportunity to express their opinions on any question of social life.

Criticism and self-criticism are a tested instrument of socialist democracy. There seems to be no open objection to this. However in real life we encounter situations indicating that by no means everyone has become aware of the need to support critical-mindedness in society. Matters at times go so far that some officials regard even the slightest remark as an encroachment upon their prestige and defend it in any way they can. Then there are those officials, the more experienced ones, who admit the justness of criticism and even thank you for it, but are in no hurry to eliminate drawbacks, expecting to get away with things as usual.

Such an attitude to criticism has nothing in common with our principles and ethics. At the present stage, when we are asserting new approaches in sociopolitical life, in the cultural and intellectual sphere, the importance of criticism and self-criticism grows immeasurably. People's attitude to criticism is an important criterion of their attitude to reorganization, to everything new that is taking place in our society. . . .

Speaking of democratization of Soviet society—which is a matter of principle to us—it is important to underline once more the main, distinguishing, feature of socialist democracy—an organic combination of democracy and discipline, of independence and responsibility, of the rights and duties of officials and of every citizen.

Socialist democracy has nothing in common with permissiveness, irresponsibility, and anarchy. Real democracy serves every person. It protects his political and social rights and simultaneously serves every collective and the whole of society, upholding their interests.

Democratization in all spheres of Soviet society is important first of all because we link it with the further development of working people's initiative and the use of the entire potential of the socialist system. We need democratization in order to move ahead, to ensure that legality grows stronger, that justice triumphs in our society and that a moral atmosphere in which man can freely live and fruitfully work is asserted in it. . . .

Today the whole world is looking at the Soviet people. Will we be able to cope with the task? Shall we hold out? Will we be able to meet worthily the challenge thrown to socialism? We must give a worthy answer by our deeds, by our persevering work. And we cannot put it off. . . .

We wish to turn our country into a model highly developed state, into a society with the most advanced economy, the broadest democracy, the most humane and lofty ethics, where the working man feels he is the real master, enjoys all the benefits of material and intellectual culture, where the future of his children is secure, where he has everything that is necessary for a full and interesting life. And even skeptics will be forced to say: yes, the Bolsheviks can accomplish anything. Yes, the truth is on their side. Yes, socialism is a system serving man, working for his benefit, in his social and economic interests, for his cultural elevation.

2

Poland, 1980–1989

Like the rest of Eastern Europe, Poland came under the control of the Soviet Union after World War II. In 1944, the Soviet Army began liberating Polish territory from the control of Nazi Germany; by 1948, Polish Communists had completed their takeover of the government, the economy, and social institutions.

Soviet leader Joseph Stalin (1879–1953) was suspicious of the Poles; he once remarked that installing his system there was like saddling a cow. Indeed, Poles did not take the saddling calmly. No society under Communist rule staged resistance more frequently than did the Poles. An armed resistance from 1944 to 1947, an uprising in 1956, a revolt by intellectuals in 1968, massive strikes in 1970 and 1976—these were just the more dramatic episodes leading up to the Solidarity experiment in 1980. Polish oppositionists in the 1980s looked to these moments of inspiration and also looked farther back to the underground state and army during World War II and to the uprisings against Russian rule in the nineteenth century. Poles, it seems, had never been willing to accept foreign or dictatorial rule. The Catholic faith that many shared (see, for example, Document 11) and that was affirmed worldwide by the election of a Pole as pope in October 1978 further encouraged resistance.

But what form of resistance was the most effective? This question reemerged with new intensity among Polish thinkers and activists during the period of martial law that followed the crushing of Solidarity in December 1981. During the first winter of martial law, slogans of rebelliousness appeared on city walls across the country: "The winter is yours, but the spring will be ours." This was a vague promise, though, because very few Poles saw value in resorting to armed uprising. Leonid Brezhnev, the Soviet leader until his death in November 1982, was the same man who had invaded Czechoslovakia in 1968 and Afghanistan in 1979 to "defend" socialism in those countries. Perhaps the Soviets would be squeamish about the possibility of massive Polish casualties—but perhaps not.

On the other hand, Poles were also practiced at waiting generations for justice. Perhaps the heroes of Solidarity, now in prison cells across Poland, would become martyrs, their names and pictures treasured secretly until a new generation would someday take up the cause. The documents in this chapter show, however, that a different scenario emerged. Polish society had been transformed by the sixteen months of relative freedom in 1980 and 1981 (see Document 8). Millions of people had gained some experience with organizing or participating in Solidarity. Many of these gave up in the face of repression, but enough stalwarts remained that the Communist leaders could not put the lid fully back on. Moreover, the economy stalled. Party leader General Wojciech Jaruzelski (1923–) had promised, in imposing martial law, that he would make the economy more efficient and would improve people's standard of living. His failure to do so undermined the passive support that Václav Havel (Document 1) and others had realized was key to Communist survival.

Three types of resistance emerged. First, there was the underground of which Adam Michnik writes in his essay (Document 9). This vast network of union organizing, self-help, and above all news—in the form of thousands of clandestinely written, edited, printed, and distributed periodicals—ensured that Solidarity and the people who fought and suffered repression were not forgotten and that they even found new allies. Second, a new generation of social movements arose, captured in Documents 10 and 11. For the most part, these were people who had not been active in Solidarity; in place of Solidarity's rhetoric evoking national traditions, they offered more prosaic ideas. Finally, Solidarity's leadership included many brilliant strategic thinkers like Jacek Kuroń (Document 12).

In the spring and summer of 1988, huge strikes broke out across Poland. Ultimately, this evidence that the Polish opposition could not be suppressed convinced the Communists to open negotiations. They hoped to draw Solidarity into taking some responsibility for the mess the regime had made of the economy. From February to April 1989, representatives of Solidarity and of the regime met at a Round Table discussion in Warsaw. The results of the Round Table included the relegalization of Solidarity, the creation of an independent newspaper, and semi-free elections to parliament. In that election, held on June 4, 1989, Solidarity candidates (including both Kuroń and Michnik) swept 99 out of 100 Senate seats and all the seats allotted to the opposition in the lower house of parliament. Less than three months later, they had wrested control of the government from the Communists, thus beginning the cascade of revolutions that would sweep the region that year.

As you read these documents, ask yourself what you learn about Polish national values from these writings. That is, when Poland or Poles are mentioned, what concepts seem to be associated with them? If they are not mentioned, do you think that fact is significant? The same question can be asked about other values, such as those related to citizenship or to Catholicism.

Another way to read these documents is as if they were in conversation with one another. For example, how do you think the participants in the actions described in Documents 10 and 11 might respond as they read Jacek Kuroń's essay (Document 12)?

8

The Solidarity Program

October 1981

Solidarity, a trade union and social movement uniting nearly ten million Poles (close to half the adult population), came into being as the result of strikes that swept Poland in July and August 1980. This was the first time that a Communist regime had allowed such an independent organization to exist. Solidarity quickly grew beyond workers to welcome white-collar professionals, students, farmers, craftspeople, and others. With its own newspaper and an entire structure of assistance to members independent of Communist control, it gave Poles—and people around the world, especially in Communist countries—hope that a space for freedom could be carved out of the dictatorship without force.

Solidarity's high point came during its National Congress in September–October 1981, at which this program was forged. Just two months later, rejecting the call for dialogue that closes the excerpt below, the Communist leaders imposed martial law on the country and detained thousands of Solidarity activists. The authors of this programmatic statement affirm both Solidarity's roots in Polish traditions and its pertinence to struggles for human and civil rights generally.

From "The Solidarity Program," in *The Solidarity Sourcebook*, ed. Stan Persky and Henry Flam (Vancouver: New Star Books, 1982), 205–7, 225.

Who We Are and What We Want

The independent, self-governing union Solidarity, which was born out of the 1980 strike, is the most powerful mass movement in the history of Poland. . . .

Our union sprang from the people's needs: from their suffering, and disappointment, their hopes and desires. It is the product of a revolt by Polish society after three decades of political discrimination, economic exploitation, and the violation of human and civil rights. It is a protest against the existing form of power.

For none of us was it just a question of material conditions— although we did live badly, working hard, often for no purpose. History has taught us that there can be no bread without freedom. We also wanted justice, democracy, truth, freedom of opinion, a reconstructed republic—not just bread, butter and sausage. . . .

Our organization combines the features of a trade union and a broad social movement; it is this which gives us our strength and determines the importance of our role. Thanks to the existence of a powerful union organization, Polish society is no longer fragmented, disorganized and lost, but has recovered strength and hope. There is now the possibility of a real national renewal. Our union, representing the majority of workers in Poland, seeks to be and will become the driving force of this renewal.

Solidarity embraces many social currents, bringing together people of different political and religious views and different nationalities. . . .

Our aim is to rebuild a just Poland.

Respect for the person must be the basis of action: the state must serve people instead of dominating them. The state organization must be at the service of society and not be monopolized by a single political party. . . .

In determining its activity, Solidarity turns to the values of Christian ethics, our national working-class tradition, and the democratic tradition of the labor world. John Paul II's encyclical on human labor[1] is a fresh source of encouragement. As a mass organization of the working people, Solidarity is also a movement for the moral rebirth of the people.

We believe that people's power is a principle that we do not have the right to abandon. But it does not mean the power of a group which places itself above society, arrogating to itself the right to define and rep-

---

[1] *Laborum Exercens* (On Human Work) was issued September 14, 1981.

resent the interests of society. Society must have the right to speak aloud, to express the range of social and political views. Society must be able to organize itself in such a way as to ensure a just distribution of the nation's material and spiritual wealth and a blossoming of all creative forces. We seek a true socialization of our government and state administration. For this reason our objective is a self-governing Poland. . . .

The Union in the Country's Present Situation

We are fully aware that Polish society expects actions from us that will allow people to live in peace. The nation will not forgive a betrayal of the ideals for which Solidarity was created. Nor will it forgive actions, even the best intentioned, which lead to the spilling of blood and the material and spiritual destruction of the country. This awareness compels us to carry out our objectives in a gradual manner, so that each consecutive action obtains the support of society.

Our sense of responsibility compels us to look with clear eyes at the relationship of forces in Europe which resulted from the Second World War. Our aim is to perform our great labor of renewal without damaging international alliances; indeed, we seek to provide more solid guarantees for those alliances. The Polish nation, animated by a sense of its dignity, patriotism and traditions, will become a valuable partner from the moment when it consciously assumes its own commitments. . . .

AGREEMENT ON ECONOMIC REFORM

Agreement on economic reform requires collaboration between the state power and society for a radical change in the existing economic order. The reform should give the leadership of enterprises to personnel within the economic system who will harmonize the laws of the market with planning. The hundreds of agreements signed by the government still remain only on paper. Promises made by the state to the working people should be honored.

AGREEMENT FOR A SELF-GOVERNED REPUBLIC

The agreement for a self-governed republic should provide the direction and means for a democratization of public life, of the *Sejm* [parliament], the political, territorial and economic authorities, the courts, national education, etc. Realization of this agreement will establish a just relationship between citizens and the state. The road to a self-governed republic is the only one which will make Poland internally strong, an equal partner with other nations.

The union considers the new social contract to be an indissoluble unity. The action program of Solidarity is above all a commitment by the union to the nation. We are confident that it will meet with the approval of the entire nation. No partisan, individual or group can consider itself to be above the nation. We do not pretend to have a monopoly on the truth. We are ready for an honest and loyal dialogue, an exchange of ideas with the state power, a quest for just decisions which will better serve the country and the interests of working people and citizens. May this accord unite us around what is national, democratic and human in Poland; around those things which do not divide us.

9

ADAM MICHNIK

On Resistance

1982

Adam Michnik (1946–), today the editor-in-chief of the Polish daily newspaper Gazeta wyborcza *("Election Newspaper"), was getting into trouble with the regime for his dissenting views even before he had graduated high school. Though he identified strongly with the left, he always connected his politics to a fierce love of Poland. He has written extensively on Polish intellectual history. While Solidarity was legal, he was one of the union's most outspoken proponents. Not surprisingly, he was interned during martial law for almost three years and was arrested again in 1985 and put on trial. This essay, written in prison in the form of a letter to an unnamed friend, appeared in English in 1985. In 1989, Michnik emerged as one of Solidarity's key negotiators with the Communists. He created Solidarity's independent daily newspaper, mobilizing people to participate in the June 1989 election.*

From Adam Michnik, "On Resistance: A Letter from Białołęka, 1982," in Adam Michnik, *Letters from Prison and Other Essays*, trans. Maya Latynski (Berkeley: University of California Press, 1985), 41, 53–58, 60–62.

My dear friend,

You have asked me how things look from this vantage point—from Białołęka prison—how I assess the effectiveness of resistance, what my projections are. . . .

You ask me whether I believe that it is sensible to maintain a political underground. . . .

No nation has ever been given human rights as a present. These rights have to be won through struggle. The question is: How should this struggle be conducted?

I am one of those who in the past ten or so years have criticized the idea of conspiratorial activity. Today I am for organizing an underground. We have no choice. Jaruzelski has made the choice for us.

This is what Polish honor and Polish thinking demand from us today. Honor: because a nation that humbly submits to those who are taking away its liberty does not deserve this liberty. Thinking: because a nation that sees no real chance for the restoration of its liberty and is not prepared to take advantage of such a chance when it arises will never attain freedom. It is difficult to be optimistic today. But who ten years ago could have foreseen the existence of a democratic opposition, an independent press, and finally August 1980 and Solidarity? It is obvious that what happened only once cannot be made into a model, but those events are an invaluable legacy. They are proof of how much can be accomplished by people who want to do something sensible for their country.

Today, the underground is a fait accompli. The forms it should take remain an open question. Let us begin by describing what it should not be. It should not be an underground state with a national government, a parliament, and armed forces. It cannot be an underground state because it has no national mandate. Our country needs many things but it does not need self-appointed national rule. It needs democratic representation—not a pseudo-parliament, which is the only thing possible in conspiratorial conditions. An underground state was able to function under the Nazi occupation because there was no middle course and because there was a war. Only a blind person could draw parallels between the General Gouvernement[1] and WRONa,[2] especially

---

[1] *General Gouvernement*: the Nazi term for the administration of occupied Poland during World War II.

[2] WRONa was the acronym for the Military Council of National Renewal that administered martial law from 1981 to 1983; *wrona* means "crow" in Polish. Michnik deliberately twists the name in contempt.

when it comes to armed conspiracy and attempts at terrorist action. This must be said clearly: armed actions could be conducted only by misguided people or by provocateurs, and the underground has a responsibility to protect society from such actions. Terrorism leads to nothing but revenge and a spiral of terror—to a strengthening of hatred and cruelty and to the estrangement of the majority of people from the underground.

It is not terrorism that Poland needs today. It is widespread underground activity that will reconstruct society, spreading throughout towns and villages, factories and research institutions, universities and high schools. Underground Solidarity has to encompass all this. . . .

Only concerted pressure, which may go as far as a general strike, can force WRONa to make concessions; this is one side of the coin. On the other side, however, is the fact that a centralized and hierarchical organization, modeled on a Leninist party, which would steer the whole national opposition, is not realistic. Life is always richer than organizational structures, and the power of an underground union organization must lie in its roots in factories and not merely in an apparatus made up of professional conspirators. Also, by its very nature, the organization must be connected to a network that goes beyond the factory, for this is indispensable in maintaining links between different groups in society, in publishing independently, in organizing internal union structures, and in organizing distribution of fliers. But if such an organization is detached from those who are living the everyday life of martial law, it can easily lose touch with reality and become an army of generals without soldiers. . . . For the activists must understand that an underground movement makes sense only when it is able to create forms of action accessible to every single Pole, when it remains an open and tolerant movement, and it always remembers that many roads lead to democracy—that the Polish national anthem can be played on many different pianos. . . . We must look for ways to develop civil society and not just undertake actions simply in order to be a nuisance to the "junta."

But, above all, we must create a strategy of hope for the people, and show them that their efforts and risks have a future. The underground will not succeed in building a widespread national opposition without such a strategy—without faith in the purpose of action. Otherwise, resistance will amount to nothing more than a moral testimony or an angry reaction. And the movement will cease to be one that is aware of its political goals, that is armed with patience and consistency, and that is capable of winning. . . .

Underground Solidarity's basic goals are obvious: to create an authentic society, a free Poland, and individual freedom in Poland. No political miracle will help the Poles if they do not help themselves. A Polish democratic state will never be born if democratic structures do not exist beforehand in Polish society. And independent of the institutional success of the underground, a base for Polish democracy *is* being created today. It lies in the moral sphere. . . .

Two strategies deserve to be considered: the strategy of "instant change" and the strategy of the "long march." The former assumes a vehement and spontaneous explosion of society's discontent. Such an explosion, even if it is bloodily suppressed, can lead to polarization within the government and restore the possibility of compromise with Solidarity. The underground must be prepared for both the quake itself and the subsequent negotiations. It must figure out ways of preventing bloodshed and ways of backing rightful demands. . . .

But this does not mean that we should bank on a head-on collision between the underground and the government for the success of our efforts. Today, any confrontation must lead to tragedy, since WRONa is full of determination and will not back down even if it means shedding rivers of blood. . . .

The "long march" strategy requires consistency, realism, and patience. These are not platitudes. They define a program of arduous, risky, and often ineffective activity, in the face of repression and suffering—a vision of work on economic, administrative, legal, and educational reform and on spreading among the public a concept of a "reformist Poland." The level of public awareness will determine the effectiveness of these actions. . . .

The underground will never meet all society's needs for a movement of resistance. It can only be one part of this movement, and the national interest requires us to seek a common denominator for different types of activity, different temperaments, and different models of concern for our motherland. The movement of resistance must teach freedom and democracy. The movement's character will determine the character of Poland as it emerges from the state of war. But the shadow of the "possessed" from Dostoyevski's novel[3] looms over every underground movement. Every conspiracy demoralizes. In its depths flourishes the spirit of a sect that uses a language all its own,

---

[3] *Dostoyevski's novel*: *The Possessed*, also known as *The Demons* (1872), a novel about revolutionary conspirators by Fyodor Dostoyevski (1821–1881).

that is based on rites of initiation, on tactics to which everything is subordinated, on an instrumental attitude toward truth, and on disregard for any values that are not political. There is a unique type of activist-conspirator, whose characteristics make him as useful in the underground as they are dangerous later on. Such an activist has to make arbitrary decisions, to distrust newcomers and strangers. A spirit of democracy is not one of the virtues required by a conspiracy; pluralism is not the style favored by it. Underground activity isolates people from the taste and smell of everyday life, skews perspectives, gives birth to dangerous absolutism and intolerance. Conspiracy requires disobedience to the enemy and obedience to the underground central command. It proclaims equality but within itself calls for hierarchical subordination. Conspiracy thrives on the spirit of Manichaeism.[4] "He who is not with us is against us." . . .

The conspirator idealizes the underground, which is not surprising, but this is precisely why he must constantly be reminded that it is not police terror that will bring about real defeat but the hostile indifference of society. An underground that is detached from a base is doomed to become degenerate and weak. . . .

The underground must know how to interpret society's needs and find flexible means of satisfying them. It must be attractive to people and it must be essential to them. These are platitudes; to adhere to them, however, we must make it clear to ourselves and to others that it is unrealistic to count on a return to the situation that preceded December 13, 1981,[5] to count on a spectacular victory, with virtue rewarded and vice punished. Underground Solidarity must not seek revenge but rather a democratic alternative. Democracy is neither an easy nor a straightforward solution. It is born in pain, strengthened in conflict; it only shows its virtues after a long time. This is why we should not promise the sky to ourselves and to others, for it is not an instant and definitive solution for Poland's troubles that awaits us but only risk, toil, and disappointment. This is usually the price of freedom.

It seems to me that the underground today does not need the moral principles and organizational structures of an army or a party of the Leninist kind. What it needs is the bond of shared aims and solidarity in action. And respect for individuality. And consent for plurality. It seems to me that the underground should not promise a world devoid of conflict. I think that it should suggest a program of practical

---

[4] *Manichaeism*: an ancient belief system. Michnik uses the term to indicate a black-and-white worldview in which the forces of good battle the forces of evil.

[5] *December 13, 1981*: the date of the imposition of martial law.

activity for reform, a program for social self-defense, contacts with real culture and cultural values, participation in authentic civic and intellectual life. Plus a pinch of dignity, a pinch of fraternity. And a daily breath of truth. Of the truth that every compromise is temporary, that every political solution is illusory. Because, as a philosopher wrote, but for death, all solutions are illusory. This is what I think.

10

WALDEMAR FYDRYCH

The Revolution of the Elves

June 1987

The Orange Alternative, a guerrilla-art collective, emerged in the southwestern city of Wrocław in 1987. It had no political program and no organization, yet by creating opportunities for free politicized expression, it quickly became the most talked-about phenomenon of Polish opposition. Its participants were students at the university, high school students, artists, musicians, and hippies; among them was Waldemar Fydrych, a thirty-four-year-old who styled himself "Major" and often dressed in military green. The Orange Alternative had staged small "happenings"—absurdist street art or performance art—since 1981. For example, participants painted little elves on walls, in places where the police had painted over political graffiti. The elves came to life in Orange Alternative's celebration of Children's Day, an actual Polish holiday, in June 1987.

Reading this document, which consists of the text of a leaflet distributed the week before the happening plus "Major" Fydrych's account of the event, it is important to avoid overanalyzing it. After all, Orange Alternative sought constantly to subvert any political meaning. Still, this and other happenings broke through the indifference to politics, exacerbated by economic crisis, that many Poles felt at this time. By engaging in ridiculous and yet accessible acts, they invited Poles to enjoy themselves again in public and to lose their fear of the police and the regime.

From Waldemar Fydrych and Bogdan Dobosz, *Hokus-Pokus, czyli Pomarańczowa Alternatywa* (Wrocław: Kret, 1989), 47–51. Translated by Padraic Kenney.

Leaflet

The elf has played an important role in world history. This creature, who lives in the forests and in books, feeding on mosses, mushrooms, and wild strawberries, is little known. . . . Elves who work in mines, in forestry, or looking after princesses and orphans are real hardworking folks. The *krasnoludek*—"krasny" meaning red, from the color of their caps, and "ludek," or little person—constitutes an important problem at the global and local scale. . . .

In the Polish People's Republic elves are not something seldom seen, but appear quite frequently. They will appear in Wrocław on Świdnicka Street by the clock at 3 p.m. on June 1. Perhaps the elf will turn out to be a great patron and friend of . . . economic reform. Others argue that the elf might be the result of those reforms.

Come! You are no worse than a princess or an orphan. Poland has a future. Long live surrealism. May the global forces of peace blossom in the shade of the military arts. . . . P.S.: Let no one be surprised if some of the elves appearing on Świdnicka Street are enormous like Gulliver. This strange mutation was caused by the explosion in a certain nuclear power plant,[1] which released heavy isotopes (cesium and strontium) that have been absorbed by mushrooms and forest undergrowth, elves' preferred food. Probably further explosions will allow us to breed with these pleasant creatures. Try to bring your own red cap.

Waldemar Fydrych's Account

This leaflet appeared in many public places . . . [and] mobilized the police. The strategic forces and rapid-response divisions turned their attention to Świdnicka Street. . . . The police know very well that in this city there are more intelligent people than modest ones. At 3:00, a none-too-modest parade marches down Szewska Street. There is a huge bear in dark glasses, festooned in toilet paper, and a sign carried by elves. On the sign is a picture of an elf, with a hole where the face should be (anyone can stick his or her face in and be photographed like an elf). Bravo! Finally the Secret Police can investigate something more colorful than the gloomy underground. . . . At 3:00 two officers go on the attack. They arrest the sign. . . . The action begins.

---

[1]The nuclear power plant at Chernobyl in the Soviet Union (in what is today Ukraine) suffered an explosion on April 26, 1986, sending a radioactive cloud over Poland.

Children's Day, June 1, 1987, Wroclaw, Poland.
The Orange Alternative's "happening" at first seems spontaneous: People are singing and dancing in a circle. But the presence of the guitar player (Krzysztof Jakubczak, one of the organizers) and the red caps worn by many remind us that even the most frivolous-seeming protest needs coordination and structure.
NAF Dementi.

Someone hands out red caps—and is detained. It's red all over, with new red caps. Here come three more policemen. An elf is handing out candy and finds himself in a police van. Another van pulls up, next to a crowd of elves as big as Gulliver. . . .

Now it's five after three. They're leading away a guy carrying bags of candy—he's still throwing handfuls to the crowd. A guitar strikes up. . . . The elves are dancing, weaving a dance line that bumps up against the police vans. Some elves knock on the windows of the van, greeting those sitting inside. The crowd presses closer, and a group starts a cheer like at a football stadium: "Elves are real!" . . .

Now there are two or three hundred elves. There are more and more caps. The crowd fills Świdnicka Street. So it's a revolution. . . .

A laugh comes from one of the police vans; a fat elf opens the door and two others jump out, throwing handfuls of candy. The elf with the guitar sings "O Rosemary Mine."[2] The crowd is partying. . . . Two elves run up to the policemen—but they don't want any candy. . . .

Now the police turn on their megaphones. . . . "Please disperse! Those who do not take off their caps must show their identity cards! Please take off the red caps!"

They arrest the guitar player. . . .

"Mommy, why are they arresting the elves?"

"Because there are no elves in the socialist system, only in capitalism," answers Mommy. . . .

"Now the reds are by the Opera—please send in the blues," reports a secret policeman. . . . The blues surround the reds—and now there are no more reds. . . .

And what will happen next time? Next time we'll have another success.

The policemen have managed to become legend: a fairy tale not just for children, but for elves, too. . . . For the first time, elves and people can compare their fairy tales as they happen.

---

[2]*"O Rosemary Mine"*: a popular love song dating to World War I.

11

The Hardest Thing to Overcome Was Our Own Foolishness . . .

June 1988

Freedom and Peace, or WiP, was one of the most powerful social movements to emerge in Poland after 1981. Students opposed to Communist control of the military founded it in 1985. They quickly expanded their activities to focus on environmental problems as well. In a country that had been driven to panic by the Chernobyl explosion of 1986, nuclear power was a potent issue.

In this document from a WiP underground paper, a woman from Międzyrzecz in northwest Poland recalls how the efforts in her small town to oppose the construction of a radioactive waste dump (in concrete bunkers built by Nazi Germany) benefited from the brazen support of WiP students from a nearby city. She shows how one small action can lead to another and how such actions can lead to concrete changes—in this case, to a decision by the Communist-controlled town council to oppose its bosses in Warsaw and refuse the construction of the waste site. Although actions by intellectuals and trade union leaders in Warsaw or other capital cities across the Communist bloc got all the attention, the self-organizing efforts in small towns like Międzyrzecz were crucial to building people's confidence in their ability to bring about change.

Międzyrzecz, beside the fact that it is a small town, a bit settled and moldy in its ways, also has a rather special population. One-third of the town is military, one-third police, and one-third are what I would call normal people. That two-to-one ratio is rather intimidating, but these are the conditions we faced. The whole thing played out spontaneously, without calculation; there were no expectations. In this environment, it wouldn't have been possible to do things differently.

Theoretically, the matter was clear. No one in Międzyrzecz, at least in private conversations, supported the storage site, but those were

From "'Najtrudniej było nam przekroczyć własną śmieszność . . .' O międzyrzeczanach międzyrzeczanki opowieść z taśmy spisana," *Pismo ruchu 'Wolność i Pokój'* (Szczecin), no. 4 (Winter 1988): 19–21. Translated by Padraic Kenney.

only discussions at home. No one from Międzyrzecz would go out onto the street to manifest dissent.

We began by forming a committee—we gathered a few people (only sixteen)—and wanted to work administratively, by lodging protests. Of course, the authorities de-legalized our committee immediately, even though it did not even have legal status yet. . . .

The whole time we wanted to act openly and not engage in some conspiratorial discussions, creating new micro-organizations. We knew that we had to go out normally onto the streets and act so that people would dare to protest aloud. Our first action was a success, though there were more onlookers than people who were genuinely engaged. After that, there were crises, too. In July [1987], for example—I consider that a disaster. A tiny little group marched. I don't know if this was because of the summer vacation or because of intimidation (by then the secret police had begun to do its thing).

At this critical moment, the boys from Gorzów's WiP helped us enormously. They began to organize pickets, which really emboldened people. . . . September came, and thanks to the boys from WiP, who picketed for two hours in the very center of town, the issue gathered steam, and something in people began to crack. After two hours, when those guys left the square, people did not allow them to be arrested. So they joined the crowd and marched through the streets with their banners, all the way to the church, where they thanked the crowd. Only after leaving the church were they detained. This action, by six boys from Gorzów's WiP, was on September 2, and then on September 6 there was a really large, successful demonstration: Then people marched with conviction. Thirty-two people were detained then. Of them, sixteen were young people who were beaten up at the police station. They tried various methods on the people they detained. One boy, for example, was stretched out on a desk while they pounded him in the kidneys. He had to get examined by a doctor, but his mother didn't want to file a complaint.

After this demonstration, twenty-five people were also fined, ranging from 25 to 40,000 złotys.[1] October 4 was the date planned for our next demonstration, and the misdemeanor court was scheduled for October 2.

The misdemeanor court came as a real shock in small-town Poland, especially since about half the people charged were chance

---

[1] Equivalent to two to three months' salary at the time.

bystanders (the other half were Solidarity activists). And then, in addition, repressive measures began about a week before the court proceedings.... After the misdemeanor court handed down the fines, doubts and lack of faith in the value of taking action once again threatened to overcome us. The hardest thing is to convince people that their voice matters in the world in which we live and that their going out onto the streets can matter. People felt ridiculous, and threatened, and played for fools, but they did not feel that they mattered.

Meanwhile, the authorities unleashed a full assault. For about a week and a half there were open meetings in workplaces, at which they tried to persuade people that dangerous political forces were directing the protest actions. There were also meetings with the parents of high school students and special pedagogical consultations. Young people were informed that there could be bloodshed and that any student who took part in a demonstration would be expelled from school.

People reacted wonderfully. A couple of these meetings were simply broken up. Women were especially radical.... But the situation was no joke; the misdemeanor court could pacify the community. They tried various things to cause fear. For example, the Gorzów press published an article, shortly before the planned demonstration, entitled "The Police Are Not Angels," in which there was a discussion about how the police sometimes have to use firearms.

On the other hand, we knew that there was an intense discussion on the topic of Międzyrzecz, and we knew we couldn't let the matter die. So we decided on a hunger strike. This was not an easy decision. The hardest thing was to overcome our own sense of foolishness: to go beyond the role that one plays (in a small town, it is hard to escape the role in which you're cast). It is really hard to shrink: One's ambitions have to shrink to nothing, especially since no one had any experience or certainty as to how it would turn out. We also could not be sure how people would respond to the hunger strike. A small town can be cruel in its criticism; we were really afraid that we would end up looking like lunatics. This was a stressful situation, as we did not know if we would have the moral strength to take this on, or if we would just look ridiculous....

None of us was completely convinced about the hunger strike. That is, we believed in the value of doing it, but we had real doubts about the form of protest. Only after two or three days did we come to feel that it has to work. People created such an atmosphere; they came to thank us, to talk, to show that they approved of what we were doing.

So this was also a moral victory: We were afraid of looking ridiculous, and instead we encountered gratitude and approval. The responsibility began to weigh upon us. One of us commented: "Even if we were to die here, we can't back out."

Our hunger strike was a complete surprise, and so people's support was both authentic and enthusiastic. The hunger strike was in protest of repression, against the approaching misdemeanor court; we condemned the issuing of such severe sanctions and demanded that civil courage be respected. . . .

We sent protest letters to the Provincial Governor and to the City Council. Our City Council, which had so far been silent, held a debate halfway through our hunger strike (on the fourth day). They met until four in the morning and, against the position of the [Communist party] first secretary, passed a resolution rejecting the decision to store radioactive materials in the bunkers and sent that resolution to the State Council. . . .

On Sunday, at noon after Mass, we were supposed to end our hunger strike and leave the church. There was a discussion: Should we exit with our banners, or without? . . . The city was dead. Other than police in their vehicles, there was no one. At each of the morning masses there were 15 to 20 people. We felt that we had lost; but then at quarter to twelve crowds of people began streaming into the church. And then, as we left the church, people's enthusiasm was enormous. Despite the fact that there was a lot of police, despite the fines, prohibitions, and intimidation, entire families came, with grandmothers and children. This was a moral victory, a civil disobedience. People greeted us with flowers, they cheered, they sang. . . . Most of all, they really weren't afraid, there was no sense of fear. . . .

One of my friends says that in our current situation one has to give people concrete activity; one should not create far-reaching, abstract ideals, but give them concrete matters to be resolved. In a small town, there is a certain kind of political awareness, and you have to work within that. If you hang banners saying, "We don't want a nuclear power plant in Żarnowiec,"[2] of course that will elicit people's approval, but it won't draw people out onto the street. Now in Międzyrzecz, the social energy has accumulated, certain habits have been broken. That's the moral value of the whole affair. People have come together

---

[2]The Polish government had begun building a nuclear reactor at Żarnowiec, on the Baltic Sea coast. Protest brought a halt to construction in 1990.

and raised up their heads. They have mobilized themselves from within. . . .

A kind of new model of resistance has been born in Międzyrzecz. It's a kind of conscious citizenship and an experience in social self-organization. Until now, activism was the normal, spontaneous kind; now we have to work it out theoretically, so as not to waste that energy. We'll have lectures and discussions, to show people that there can be two or three theories on one topic (for example, on social movements). The point of all this is to embolden people and to work out methods of conscious disobedience. . . .

The open meetings in workplaces were more than just angry encounters; they were demonstrations. People stood up and told those secret police and party bosses that they are swindlers. At the meeting with high school parents, for example, parents stood up and said that they don't care about all these prohibitions and injunctions, because the lives of their children are more important to them. . . .

Above all, we have to come out of our hiding places. Certain activities have to become public if they are going to be effective. Nothing will be taken care of if we do not come out and demonstrate our citizenship.

12

JACEK KUROŃ

Instead of Revolution
March 8, 1989

In this document, Polish dissident Jacek Kuroń (1934–2004) reports on the negotiations at the Round Table for the leading underground weekly newspaper. Kuroń was considered by many to be Solidarity's foremost strategic thinker. Like Adam Michnik, he spent many years in prison for his tireless defense of the freedom to organize and the freedom of speech.

From Jacek Kuroń, "Zamiast rewolucji," *Tygodnik Mazowsze*, March 8, 1989. Published in *Okrągły Stół. Dokumenty i materiały*, vol. 3, ed. Włodzimierz Borodziej and Andrzej Garlicki (Warsaw: Kancelaria Prezydenta Rzeczypospolitej Polskiej, 2004), 379–82. Translated by Padraic Kenney.

After the bloody uprisings of the 1970s, Kuroń exhorted the people of Poland: "Don't burn down committees, but form your own!" That is, instead of attacking Communist party headquarters and burning it down in rage, they should organize themselves. Once a radical, Kuroń had by 1989 become a hardheaded realist seeking to wrest concessions from the Communists. He saw the Round Table as a step toward Solidarity's taking power but came to the conclusion that Solidarity would have to cooperate with its opponents for the good of Poland. Here he takes on the task of convincing Solidarity's enthusiastic supporters to accept compromise.

Our deliberations are in the Office of the Council of Ministers—that is, in the ruler's palace. Oppositionists enter palaces either at the head of an armed people, in order to take power away, or at the invitation of the ruler who wants to consolidate his power. Can the opposition agree to such an invitation? Yes, if it will therefore have a greater likelihood of accomplishing its program.

Some of those in the ruling elite have lately realized that the current system of exercising power is lethal: The destruction of the country will sooner or later lead to their own destruction. They probably hope that they can manage to stabilize a more efficient system, with themselves at the top. To achieve this, however, they have to take the path of democratic changes. And thus there emerges a sphere of mutual interests.

There are some people who accuse us: You're propping up the regime when of course it would be better to wait a little longer and ride a wave of strikes and demonstrations into the palace. That is, at the head of an armed people. I won't get into whether we could win. Let's even assume that such a possibility exists. The thing is, however, that dozens of revolutions have already taken place around the world. It's an old fairy tale: People place all their hopes in a revolution, and those hopes cannot be fulfilled. There always comes a crisis and hatred: The first revolutionaries are swept away by their successors, until finally one of these successor groups uses violence against the people. There have not been other kinds of revolutions. And thus, ever since I stopped being a Communist and a very young man, I have ceased to advocate revolution. Today a revolution would be many times worse: We've got, after all, a ruined country, and through revolution we would not only fail to rebuild it but would ruin it further. All the problems that we have now would rise up before us with even greater force.

I don't deny that it may turn out that there is no other way. But we have a responsibility to attempt a process in which the entire society will organize itself and change the present order gradually. The task of people who engage in politics is to do everything to pursue process instead of coup d'état.

Despite the popular belief that there is no point in talking with Communists, I would like to declare that not only is it possible, but we in fact have no choice.

Does this mean that I trust the regime—that I propose that we have confidence in the *nomenklatura*,[1] the bureaucracy, the party? Well, I am against any mixing of one's social life and politics. I can have confidence in my friends, but in politics one should follow the principle that power is the only guarantor. . . .

Our basic demand at the Round Table is for the right to organize; here we have achieved a great deal. We also need access to mass media, which makes it possible not only to organize, but also to communicate among ourselves, independently of the regime. . . .

The regime tells us that it requires a guarantee that organized social forces will not overthrow the government or tear down the system. And it does not seek these guarantees in the form of pledges or self-limiting from our side but in the parliamentary system. It demands that we participate in parliamentary elections, which would be much more democratic than before, but still nondemocratic. This would of course place limitations on the independent forces, because entry into parliament imposes on us responsibility for the state. Recently they have added the creation of a presidency with quite broad powers and a Senate chosen by genuinely free elections to their proposal.

If it does turn out to be possible to set democratic processes in motion, then it seems to us that this contract can only be accepted as a one-time deal; we would declare quite clearly that the next elections would have to be free. I have often been asked what guarantee we have that the next elections will be free. I think that is a silly question. . . . The only real guarantee, in fact, is an organized society. To the extent society is able to transform the actual situation, so too it will be able to bring about free elections. . . .

It is worth recalling that when our side entered the talks it thought: We'll get Solidarity back, and maybe something else, and we'll pay for

---

[1] *nomenklatura*: the Communist elite, who held key positions in the state administration and in the economy.

it with undemocratic elections. Now we have the Solidarity we wanted.... A change in Solidarity's philosophy has occurred; we understood that the point of these talks is not to snatch something for ourselves, but to get the whole process moving. . . .

What will happen if the agreement breaks down: If society rejects it *in toto* for economic reasons? If the decisive piece of paper is not the ballot, but the ration card? It is not an accident that at assemblies in factory I talk about Parliament, the Senate, and the elections, and people ask about wage hikes and price hikes. . . . But I don't believe in the primitive class vision: that if someone is a steelworker in the Lenin [Steel] Mill, then he sees nothing beyond his position in the mill. Experience, especially the experience of Solidarity, shows that this is not true. One is also a consumer, a citizen, a Pole. And this means that we can overcome the resistance to economic change.

We face a problem: Are we capable of conducting this transformation from totalitarianism to democracy peacefully? Someone said to me: In four years, Solidarity will win the elections anyway, and the Communists will lose [and so why bother to negotiate?][2] This way of thinking is as if today's situation would still hold four years from now. But we have the opportunity to create a completely new political geography, favoring the stabilization of a democratic system over the course of those four years. In four years, Solidarity and the Communist Party will not be opposing each other. I think that the party will split up, and so will the opposition.

Besides, one cannot think about free elections like a revolution. If one side loses in a revolution, it does not rebuild, unless the revolution itself fails. But if a party loses an election, it might win in four years— and if not in four years, then in eight.

What is happening in Poland—and it must be happening with Gorbachev's approval—is a decisive experiment for the [Soviet] Bloc. Gorbachev faces the same problem . . . : Can one reach an agreement with the opponents of totalitarianism?[3] . . .

---

[2]The agreement eventually signed at the Round Table called for partially free elections in 1989, and free elections—that is, with each seat in parliament contested—in 1993. This point was moot by the end of 1989.
[3]Mikhail Gorbachev revoked the so-called Brezhnev doctrine that justified the inva-
~ of allied countries. Kuroń suggests that Gorbachev's efforts to reach out to reform-
~ment 7) are analogous to the challenges that the Polish Communists face
willingness of Polish Communists to negotiate can be in part explained by
, openness to experimentation within the Soviet Bloc.

Of course, there is the possible scenario in which the Soviet Union collapses. In that situation, we will build independence and democracy from the ground up. In a system in which there is a fundamental chasm between rulers and society, any revolution and total transformation result in completely unprepared people coming to power and governing the state and the economy. If we succeed at the Round Table in overcoming that chasm in some places, then the collapse of the system will be less dangerous because there will be more directors, administrators, bureaucrats, judges who are reasonable. The greater a social accord we achieve today—in the sense that we trust this or that judge, director, or minister—the easier will it be for us to cross over to a new system.

Yesterday we still stood in the trenches of two opposing armies, which fired upon each other and destroyed everything in their path. Today a completely new social, political, psychological situation has arisen.

3

The Philippines, 1983–1986

Until the Philippines underwent a democratic revolution in the mid-1980s, there were two ways in which a dictatorship like that of Ferdinand Marcos (1917–1989) could come to an end. Many such regimes fell when military officers executed a coup after becoming dissatisfied with the inefficiencies and corruption of a longtime dictator whom they had once supported. This change of leadership sometimes led to reform but often merely produced a new dictatorship. The other engine of political change—and Cuba (1959) is the classic example—was a popular insurgency. The guerrillas might or might not have much interest in Communist ideology, but the cold war helped channel their demands into this familiar form.

Both outcomes were plausible in the Philippines, where the insurgent groups were quite strong—and in fact remained so well after 1986. The threat of Communist guerrilla forces also ensured that the military would continue to be crucial to Marcos's rule. The strong U.S. presence only underscored the idea that the Philippines were on the front lines of the cold war. The island nation had been a U.S. colony until 1946. Throughout the cold war, two huge military bases and several smaller ones reminded Filipinos just how important their country and its leader were to the United States, and fueled their suspicions of American intentions.

Ferdinand Marcos, then fifty-five and Philippine president since 1965, used the Communist insurgency as an excuse to declare martial law in 1972. Marcos abolished Congress and threw many senior opposition politicians, including Senator Benigno Aquino, into prison. Only in 1980, under pressure from the United States, did Marcos formally relax martial law. In reality, however, he continued his tight control over politics and society while draining the country of billions of dollars for his private enrichment. By 1983, the once-vibrant economy ˙ ˙ᵈ taken a nosedive. Marcos, meanwhile, was gravely ill, and military ˙ ˙ˢsibly with the involvement of First Lady Imelda Marcos) ing to control the succession. Benigno Aquino decided to return from exile to lead the fight for democracy but was assassinated as he stepped off the plane in Manila on August 21, 1983.

The succession crisis should have doomed the Philippines to a bloody future. That it did not stems from three main factors. First, the Catholic Church and its leader, Cardinal Jaime Sin, took an unambiguous and explicit position both against the Marcos regime—a stand that the Church did not take in many other dictatorships—and in favor of nonviolent change. Along the way, Cardinal Sin elevated Benigno Aquino into a martyr for Philippine democracy. Second, Aquino's widow, Corazon (Cory) Aquino[1] (1933–2009), immediately announced that she would return home for her husband's funeral. Surprisingly, she emerged as a strong force for reconciliation rather than revenge. Though lacking political experience, she soon began to speak out about human rights and democracy.

The third factor was what Filipinos called "the Parliament of the Streets." Within four days of Benigno Aquino's assassination, several left-wing senators, supported by business allies in Manila and by Aquino's brother, created JAJA—Justice for Aquino, Justice for All. JAJA staged dozens of innovative protests and demonstrations that fall. The following spring, when Marcos called for parliamentary elections, a monitoring group called the National Movement for Free Elections (NAMFREL) formed with the purpose of watching every polling place. Its founder, Jose Concepcion, was close to Cardinal Sin, and the organization drew many of its 150,000 volunteers (not enough, in the end, to prevent fraud) from the business community. This awakening of the middle/entrepreneurial class also contributed to the successful avoidance of the more violent alternatives mentioned earlier.

By the end of 1985, then, Filipinos had some two years' experience in civil society, at least in urban areas. The Church was now well integrated into opposition politics, too. Finally, Marcos had lost much of his support, except in Washington, where President Ronald Reagan remained a strong advocate until the very end. On the other hand, one legacy of Marcos's years in power was many long-thwarted ambitions among the political elite—and thus deep divisions in the opposition. That November, confident that he would be able to maintain power, Marcos called for a presidential election to be held in February.

---

[1] Filipino politics is quite informal and marked by nicknames for everyone. Benigno Aquino was universally known as Ninoy.

Corazon Aquino announced her intention to run for president. Opposing her was Senator Salvador Laurel, the leader of the parliamentary opposition and thus the heir apparent. Many observers believe that the key moment in Marcos's downfall came when Cardinal Sin persuaded Laurel to put aside his ambitions and run instead as Aquino's vice presidential candidate. This development cleared the field for a one-on-one contest in which Ferdinand Marcos was cast in the role of a usurper with blood on his hands.

At the height of the protests, British journalist James Fenton records a proud Filipino exclaiming, "We've beaten Poland," thinking of how Solidarity had fallen short of victory a few years before.[2] Indeed, the Filipino revolution was part of a loosely connected chain of revolutionary events. Almost two years later, protesters in South Korea waved their hands in the Philippine *L* sign (for *Laban*, "fight," the name of Benigno Aquino's political party in the 1970s) as they demonstrated against their authoritarian leader. The toppling of a dictator by peaceful means was also instructive for other societies in East and Southeast Asia, including Taiwan (1992), Thailand (1992), and Indonesia (1998).

In reading these documents, consider these questions: What kinds of people are engaged in the protest actions proposed and described in the selections? Are they similar to those active in Poland? And would you say that the protests and the revolution itself, as portrayed in the documents, emphasized *rejection* of the old regime or *advocacy* of a new political order?

.on, *All the Wrong Places: Adrift in the Politics of the Pacific Rim* (New ₫onthly Press, 1988), 198.

13

Primer of the "Justice for Aquino, Justice for All" Movement

September 1983

From August 1983, immediately after Benigno (Ninoy) Aquino's assassination, through mid-1984, JAJA staged dozens of events, some of which sound like the "happenings" of Orange Alternative (Document 10). Demonstrators marched through the streets of the Philippine capital, Manila, amid showers of confetti tossed by office workers ripping up paper; citizens created "noise barrages" by banging on pots and honking horns to make their protest heard; there was even a parade of dogs dressed up in opposition T-shirts. This last event featured the slogan "Bark for Benigno, Howl for Hope." Although the document below does not tell about any of these events, it illustrates JAJA's main demands and illuminates the organization's background.

Beginnings

"JAJA" is the acronym of the Justice for Aquino, Justice for All Movement. It was launched on August 25, 1983 by organizations advocating the abolition of the Presidential Commitment Order (PCO).[1] When Ninoy Aquino was assassinated, they realized that eliminating the PCO was not enough. They decided to enlarge their cause by creating JAJA. JAJA is growing rapidly: more and more organizations affiliated with it, and chapters are being formed throughout the country. As of October 15, less than two months after its creation, JAJA had nearly ninety chapters and member organizations.

JAJA is non-partisan and multi-sectoral. It is an organization of organizations, not of individuals. Its members include civic, business,

[1]*Presidential Commitment Order:* an order issued by Ferdinand Marcos in January 1981, which allowed him to order the detention of opponents.

From "Primer of the 'Justice for Aquino, Justice for All' Movement," in *Dictatorship and Revolution: Roots of People's Power,* ed. Aurora Javate de Dios, Petronilo Bn. Daroy, and Lorna Kalaw-Tirol (Manila: Conspectus, 1988), 566–68.

professional, cultural, farmers', workers', and students' organizations and other action groups devoted to public, religious, and humanitarian causes.

Credo

- The Philippines is for Filipinos, not for foreigners. For all Filipinos, not just a few. For all generations of Filipinos, not just the present generation. This can only be achieved through justice, freedom, democracy, and sovereignty.
- As long as the present regime is in power, receiving continuous U.S. military, political, and economic support, genuine freedom and democracy cannot be attained. We have no quarrel with the American people but we oppose the policies of the U.S. Government with respect to the Filipinos.
- Only a united, organized, determined, and militant Filipino people can actualize their hopes and aspirations.
- True democracy requires the active participation and representation in the government of all social sectors and classes.
- Militant, vigilant action based on truth is necessary to attain our people's quest for justice, freedom, democracy and sovereignty.

Objectives

- We demand the immediate resignation of President Marcos, the entire Cabinet, the Executive Committee, members of Batasang Pambansa,[2] and top generals of the military. A responsible transition government composed of men and women of unquestionable integrity should be established to pave the way for the realization of genuine democracy in this country.
- We demand the immediate restoration of the *Writ of Habeas Corpus* throughout the country, the immediate release of all political prisoners, and the grant of unconditional amnesty to all political dissenters and dissidents.
- We demand a fair, open, independent and impartial investigation of the assassination of Ninoy Aquino.

Pambansa: the Philippine parliament.

- We demand the complete restoration of freedom of speech, the press, of peaceful assembly, and all other constitutional rights and civil liberties.
- We demand a stop to U.S. or to any other foreign intervention in Philippine affairs.
- We demand an end to the militarization of our society and to repression and terrorism.
- We demand the restoration of the independence and integrity of the judiciary.

Programs

JAJA supports massive multi-sectoral education and information campaigns through:

- Rallies and assemblies, fora, symposia in schools, factories, offices, districts, and neighborhood communities.
- Mass demonstrations, marches, picketing, boycotts, and all forms of militant protests.
- Others forms of concerted actions such as prayer rallies, protest runs, wearing or displaying of protest symbols such as pins, stickers, posters, streamers, and other paraphernalia.
- Organization of JAJA chapters representing all social sectors and classes. . . .

Non-Partisan Nature

JAJA is not a political party. JAJA does not intend to take part in partisan activities. But its members are free to join any political party or movement provided they do so in their individual capacity and do not use the name of JAJA.

14

JAIME SIN

Guidelines on Christian Conduct during Elections
December 28, 1985

Cardinal Jaime Sin (1928–2005) was one of Pope John Paul II's closest allies and a key figure in the Filipino opposition to Ferdinand Marcos's rule. In this pastoral letter, Sin offers explicit instructions to the people. He specifically endorses the work of NAMFREL, the independent monitoring group, while also mentioning the work of COMELEC, the official election commission. This direct appeal probably contributed to an important moment two days after the February 7, 1986, vote, when several dozen computer operators walked off their jobs at COMELEC, bringing the vote tabulation, which Marcos was trying to manipulate, to a halt. The appeal is an unusual one, as religious leaders rarely intervene in a matter so clearly secular as are voting procedures.

Beloved brothers and sisters in Christ:

Peace be with you! We, your pastors, wish to speak to you about the forthcoming February 7 elections.

We all know how important these elections are. They are so decisive that their failure may plunge our country into even greater instability and violence. It is thus of the utmost importance that every voting Filipino does all in his power: 1) to vote in this election; 2) to assure that it be peaceful and honest in its conduct, and 3) to ensure that it becomes really an expression of the people's sovereign will.

We know from past experience that all this does not come about automatically. Our elections and referenda in the past 20 years have been marred by widespread violence and dishonesty. On the other hand, our experience in Metro Manila in the last elections showed that with the proper vigilance and effort the people can express their

---

Jaime L. Sin, "Guidelines on Christian Conduct during Elections," in *The Philippine Revolution and the Involvement of the Church*, ed. Fausto Gomez (Manila: UST Social Research Center, 1986), 40–44.

will effectively through the ballot, and can ensure that the truth will be respected and prevail.

We wish to emphatically point out that participation in these coming elections is not only a political act. It is also an exercise of our Christian faith. We should participate in this electoral process *as Christians*. Our faith must exercise and manifest itself in the public domain by the way we conduct ourselves during these elections. Our Christian faith must be lived not only in the privacy of our consciences and in the sanctuary of our churches but also in our effort to make our country a place where human dignity is respected and peace—the fruit of justice and love—prevails. No one should be more concerned than Christians to shape a society worthy of God's children.

Hence, was ask *all voters*:

1. Inform yourselves well of the persons and issues involved so that you can exercise an enlightened judgment in the polling places.
2. Do what you can, singly and in organized collaboration with others, to promote the election into office of worthy candidates.
3. Be sure to register, and check whether you are properly registered. Be sure you can vote on February 7.
4. Vote on February 7, and assure yourselves that your ballots are cast in the proper ballot boxes without being tampered with.
5. Stay around the precincts in organized numbers, especially during counting time, and help ensure that the votes are properly counted and tallied, all the way to the office of the COMELEC.
6. Do not cheat. Do not cast more than one ballot.
7. Do not sell your vote. The acceptance of money to vote for a candidate (a practice we do not encourage) *does not bind you to vote for that candidate*. No one is obliged to fulfill an evil contract.

To NAMFREL volunteers, and others like them:

1. We praise, support, and endorse fully your selfless efforts. The Lord will reward you as true peacemakers.
2. Our priests and concerned parishioners are willing and ready to extend to you whatever help they can to help you pursue your noble work. Do not hesitate to ask for their cooperation.

To those who will man and supervise the polls, and to the COMELEC:

1. We are hopeful that you will do your work in a truly patriotic and Christian way. Please do not fail your country and God.
2. Please remember that you are the servants of the people, and not of any one person or political party. Count and tally the votes honestly. Respect the will of the people. It is a seriously immoral and unchristian act to cheat or make others cheat during these elections. It is a serious act of injustice against your fellow Filipinos, your country, and God, who cannot be mocked.

To the candidates, political parties, and their followers:

1. We support your stated wish for clean, peaceful, and honest elections.
2. Campaign as hard as you can, but reject deceit, dishonesty, and violence during these elections.
3. Do not buy votes, coerce, or harm people in any way.
4. If you commit injustice, you will be bound to undo the damage by fitting reparation. Election violence and cheating are sins that cry to heaven for vengeance.

And finally, to all Filipinos:

So much is involved in these elections. The very future of our country is at stake. Let no one be uninvolved and indifferent. Everybody must do his share. We exhort everyone, even the children, to pray for honest and peaceful elections. We exhort those who can fast to do so for this purpose. And we exhort the sick and suffering to offer their sufferings and prayers also for this intention. By our vigilance and Christian involvement in the February 7 elections, let us prove that we are being converted to the Lord, and that there is an effective non-violent way to change the structures in our society.

May the Lord God of history lead us all to a better future through the expression of, and respect for, the people's sovereign will. May Mary our Mother accompany us with her maternal love.

Dear brothers in the priesthood:

Peace! You know how crucial for our country the February 7 elections are. It is certainly God's will that we do our part as religious leaders to help ensure that the elections be honest and peaceful, and truly expressive of the people's will. Hence, I write to you, as the pastor of this archdiocese, to ask you to do the following:

1. *Evangelize all those who are involved in the election process:* voters, the persons who will man and supervise the polls (the teachers, the COMELEC personnel, the NAMFREL people and other poll volunteers, and the members and followers of the different political parties), indeed all the people, even the sick and suffering.
   a. Do this by personal contacts, through homilies, seminars, recollections, etc.
   b. Instruct the people on the relevance of their faith to these elections (cf. enclosed pastoral letter to the people and the Bible Texts).
   c. Form core groups which will conduct or help conduct with you the said seminars and recollections.
   d. Read in all the Masses on January 1, 5, and 12, 1986, enclosed pastoral letter. Multiply copies and distribute them to your people.

2. *Encourage your parishioners to participate in the electoral process and to ensure that the polls be clean, peaceful, and reflective of the people's will.*
   a. Ask the people to enlighten themselves on the persons and issues involved in these elections, so that they may vote wisely.
   b. Ask them to work singly and in organized groups for the election of the candidates they deem worthy.
   c. Tell them to register and make sure they are registered and listed properly.
   d. Tell them to vote on February 7, and to make sure their votes are properly cast and tallied.
   e. Tell them to exercise organized vigilance in the precinct, and all the way to the COMELEC office, to make sure that the counting and tallying of votes is done honestly and accurately. Encourage them to report election violations to the media, NAMFREL volunteers, and the COMELEC.
   f. Support the NAMFREL. Encourage the formation of NAM-FREL units in your parishes. Get your parishioners to collaborate with NAMFREL.

3. *Pray and fast, and encourage your parishioners to pray and fast for peaceful and honest elections.*
   a. Pray with your people the enclosed prayer of the faithful, daily, in every Mass.

b. Encourage your parishioners to tune in to RADIO VERITAS at 6 a.m., 12 noon, and 6 p.m., for the Angelus, during which there will also be a prayer for peaceful and honest elections.

c. Hold prayer vigils (at least on February 6, 8 p.m. to 12 midnight) for honest and peaceful elections.

Dear fathers, we are not political leaders. But as religious leaders and pastors it is our duty to provide moral guidance and encouragement to our people in these times of grave crisis. Above all, we accompany and lead our people to respond as Christians concerned not only for their own conversion of heart, but for the renewal of the temporal order according to God's will. And we must encourage them to actively seek non-violent solutions to the problems that afflict us all.

May we not fail our people and God in this crucial moment of our country's history: May we be agents of hope for our people.

December 8, 1985

Sincerely in the Lord,
JAIME CARDINAL L. SIN
Archbishop of Manila
and AUXILIARY BISHOPS OF MANILA

15

The Civil Disobedience Campaign
February 1986

NAMFREL estimated that Aquino defeated Marcos by nearly one million votes, out of some fifteen million cast, despite Marcos's comment that a woman was qualified only for the bedroom. Parliament nevertheless certified Marcos as the winner. On February 14, the Catholic Bishops' Conference, an organization representing the hierarchy of the Roman Catholic Church in the Philippines, formally condemned Marcos's efforts

"Discussion Notes of the Advisory Committee for the Civil Disobedience Campaign, Makati, February 13, 1986," in *Dictatorship and Revolution: Roots of People's Power*, ed. Aurora Javate de Dios, Petronilo Bn. Daroy, and Lorna Kalaw-Tirol (Manila: Conspectus, 1988), 734–37.

to falsify the election results. Although this denunciation increased international pressure on Marcos, the way to victory was not at all clear. A military coup was a plausible outcome; so, too, was an armed conflict that might have allowed Marcos to declare martial law. On February 16, however, Corazon Aquino addressed a crowd estimated at two million, outlining a plan—which she and her advisers had laid out in the following document a few days earlier—for civil disobedience. The specific action would be a boycott of government-controlled firms, such as the ubiquitous San Miguel beer, of the government press, and even of the banks. The author of Document 16 points to the influence of Martin Luther King Jr. on this campaign.

Economic and Financial Sanctions

There are actions to be undertaken to reduce the flow of money to the government and to entities supporting the present administration. For this program to work, the massive cooperation of the citizenry is required.

It is therefore critical that the public be made fully aware just how important this aspect of the program is to the total effort to peacefully achieve change.

The principal messages that must be communicated to the public are:

1. The availability of massive amounts of cash to Marcos and his cronies is what permits them to continue with their repressive activities. Access to such funds enables them to hire goons to terrorize the citizens. It also enables them to afford operating corrupt newspapers and TV/radio stations as well as to hire sycophants to attend pro-government rallies in order to keep up the illusion of public support. Therefore, the public must cooperate in ensuring that the flow of funds to Marcos and his cronies is curtailed.
2. A disruption of economic activities will scare the international agencies (esp. foreign lending institutions) and thereby force them to apply pressure on the present government.

We must also recognize that employees of the crony companies may feel initially threatened by the boycott moves against their employers especially if many of them actually voted for the opposition against the wishes of their employers. It is therefore important that

Cory Aquino also address a message to them so as not to alienate too many of them. The message to them should perhaps be along the following lines:

1. That the sanctions are addressed mainly to hurt the owners of the crony firms and not its employees. The employees are not expected to suffer very much from the boycott because the law requires that these crony firms continue to pay them salaries and wages despite the decline in their sales and profitability.
2. While there could be some boycotted firms that might resort to laying off workers, this is not expected to be very many. Their respective labor unions should apply pressure on their managements to prevent them from resorting to this move. Should some workers be adversely affected by such moves, they should bear in mind that these are short-term sacrifices that many of us will have to make in the higher interest of the nation. In the long run, we shall all benefit under a regime of truth, freedom and social justice.

The specific actions that may be undertaken for each sector to be addressed are described below:

CRONY/GOVERNMENT BANKS

The action will have to be first taken against those crony or government banks that are known to have actively supported the regime during the elections either financially or thru the intimidation of their employees in brazen disregard of their employees' rights.

The suggested course of action will be as follows:

First, there will be a call by Cory Aquino for the public to boycott the selected banks. More specifically:

1. depositors will be asked to withdraw their deposits from said entities.
2. borrowers will be asked to delay for as long as possible payment of their loans with said banks.
3. all other banks (who are supportive of the moderate opposition) will be urged not to help the crony banks with interbank loans during their liquidity crisis.

Second, if the above action still proves inadequate after one week, organized action can be taken to disrupt the operations of the crony banks. These actions will, however, have to be peaceful and completely legal. Such actions may include organizing large groups of people to open small accounts (say P10 to P50 each) with said banks, then subsequently withdrawing from said accounts on that same day. These depositors should conduct their business with the banks as slowly as possible and should do this routine every day for two consecutive weeks.

This activity will slow down service in these banks to a crawl and thereby discourage other regular depositors from doing business with these institutions. Moreover, the long queue can scare depositors as they may interpret the long lines as a bank run.

CRONY COMPANIES

Again, as with the crony banks, a manageable number of establishments should first be selected. The list can be slowly expanded as the public gets more accustomed to the names. We can perhaps begin with San Miguel Corp., Rustan, Fortune Tobacco and Asia Brewery as well as the three prominently pro-Marcos hotels, namely: Manila Hotel, Phil. Plaza, and Hyatt.

1. Again, the first action should be a call by Cory Aquino for a complete boycott of these establishments.
2. To support this move, a comprehensive list of the products of these firms (in the case of manufacturers) should be distributed to the public for reference. Also, to keep the momentum going, stickers and leaflets can be produced for wide public distribution urging the boycott movement.
3. The top managements of business firms sympathetic to the cause of the moderate opposition should also be personally asked to support the move by refraining from sourcing their raw materials requirements from establishments that are targets of the boycott move.
4. In the case of retail/service establishments like Rustans and the hotels, further action can be taken to deter patronage by the public such as by volunteers clogging their parking areas with cars during prime shopping periods.
5. There should be constant reminders to the public of this boycott program thru daily announcements in Radio Veritas and the alternative press.

ESTABLISHMENT PRESS AND MEDIA

This has basically two components, namely:

1. A call on the public to boycott (i.e. cancel subscriptions and refrain from further purchases) all establishment newspapers, magazines and other publications; and
2. A call on all business leaders to completely stop any form of advertising with the establishment papers, all TV stations and radio stations with the exception of Radio Veritas.

Moral Pressure

This category includes all actions to be taken to put pressure on the government and those supporting the government (including foreign entities) and to diminish their credibility and moral resolve to struggle. This includes mass protest action by the public, and private pressure on government officials and on foreign entities.

MASS ACTION

This refers to demonstrations and protest rallies to be directly participated in by the public. This is the most sensitive of the activities since it is the one most fraught with risk. The government could use the mass action events to provoke violence, which may get out of the control of the organizers considering the seething anger of the population. Nevertheless, this aspect of the program is necessary as this is the best way to apply pressure and to demonstrate the clamor of the people for change.

If successful in Metro-Manila, the sit-down strikes can be expanded to the provinces and the durations can later be extended for a whole month if necessary.

The deliberate slowdown in economic activity will put pressure on the international community especially the multi-national firms doing business in the country and the international financial institutions with loans to the Philippines. They could, in turn, put pressure on their governments to denounce the current regime.

PRESSURE ON GOVERNMENT OFFICIALS

The objective of this move is to reach those officials in government who may still possess the decency to recognize that the regime they are supporting is illegitimate with the hope that they could have the courage to resign as did the heroic computer programmers of the COMELEC. A three-pronged approach can be pursued here:

1. Personal contact and appeal by people close to these officials who are sympathetic to the cause of change.
2. Letters from the public that will appeal to their sense of fairness, decency, and patriotism and call for their resignation.
3. Pickets to be organized in their places of residence to increase pressure on them to resign.

PRESSURE ON THE U.S. AND INTERNATIONAL ENTITIES

The objective of this action will be to put public opinion to bear to persuade the U.S. government, the government of other countries and other international entities that Mr. Marcos lacks the mandate of the people and that they should withdraw recognition of his government or otherwise withdraw support from him.

This can be done through a massive letter campaign from the public to be addressed to the U.S. embassy and the various foreign embassies in Manila and to *Time Magazine, Newsweek, Asian Wall Street Journal* and other international publications.

16

LEDIVINA V. CARIÑO

The Revolution of 1986: A Personal Story
1986

The boycott that Corazon Aquino called for was quite successful, but many Filipinos still felt that only a military coup could force Marcos out. One of Marcos's close allies, Secretary of Defense Juan Enrile, was known to have switched sides; he was abruptly joined by police chief Lieutenant General Fidel Ramos. Under threat of attack by Marcos's forces, Enrile and Ramos appealed for public support.

Everything changed quite suddenly on the evening of February 22, when Cardinal Sin appealed on Radio Veritas—the Catholic Church's station, whose broadcaster June Keithley became a symbol of courage during

From Ledivina V. Cariño, "The Revolution of 1986: A Personal Story," manuscript.

the revolution—for people to heed Enrile and Ramos's call. The cardinal's pleas had the effect of taking the initiative away from the military and putting it in the hands of ordinary people, including many priests and nuns, who blocked the streets, even kneeling in front of armored vehicles. The result, beginning on the night of February 22–23, was a massive display of civil disobedience—of people power, as it came to be known. The four-day occupation of the highway in front of the army barracks culminated in Marcos's departure, in an American helicopter, on the evening of February 25. This document is a narrative of those hours, written down shortly thereafter by Ledivina V. Cariño, a sociologist at the University of the Philippines (UP). Cariño's account reveals both amazement that a peaceful revolution could take place and pride in her fellow Filipinos.

"Dawn is breaking. Dawn is breaking. Please stay in your posts. Don't leave. Tear gas will not destroy us now. Here is the National Anthem to sustain you."

It is early morning of Monday, February 24, 1986. The voice is that of June Keithley. The station is unknown. I found the band by accident after a dreadful night hardly sleeping, discouraged that Marcos seems to have won again. . . .

June was talking to the defenders of EDSA[1] to stay put as tanks approached and they were tear-gassed while gunships flew noisily and menacingly overhead. She had stayed up all night, but she still managed to say the right words. . . . My tears started to flow as she played "Bayan Ko," (My Country, the song of the opposition), and then she faltered in a prayer. "Lord," she said, "I do not know how to do this but please, please stay with us," or words to that effect. "Dawn is about to break." Then she called for first aid, medical assistance. I woke Ben up. Marcos was moving in with his troops. It was going to be violent after all.

The helicopter gunships continued circling the Aguinaldo area. My heart stopped. They were really going to slaughter us! Then June's jubilant voice: "They are defecting. They are joining the Reformists!" Hallelujah! . . . Why Marcos didn't or couldn't shut down the station or the telephones probably showed his impotence best. . . .

That morning, we still did not call it a "revolution." . . . On the way to the office, we heard the news: the reformists were taking Channel 4,

---

[1]*EDSA*: Epifanio de los Santos Avenue, the major highway skirting the core of metropolitan Manila.

Filipino Soldier and Civilians.

Flowers have long been used as counter-weapons in peaceful protests. In Prague in 1968, Czech students placed them in the barrels of the guns of Soviet soldiers; protesters at the Pentagon in 1967 did the same thing. Thus it is hard to say whether these Filipinas recognized the universal resonance of their action, caught in this photo from February 1986.

Photograph by John K. Chua.

supported as usual by the people, many of whom probably walked all the way from EDSA. . . . Nora Romblon, one of our researchers, informed me of a general assembly of UP Manila at the Little Theater. . . . The theater was almost full, mostly undergrads from their College of Arts and Sciences, but also some medical students, nurses and dental students in bright yellow T-shirts that said FIGHT TRUTH DECAY. Minda Luz Quesada of the Institute of Public Health was presiding. She is an activist nurse and an old friend. She was probably the only person above 35 until I entered the room. . . . She asked if I could help analyze the situation.[2] . . . Whatever were the actual facts, our position

[2]Elsewhere in her memoir, Cariño writes, "At the time of the Ramos-Enrile defection, I was making a proposal for what else to boycott and their timing, an assignment from Dr. [Jovito] Salonga [1920– , a leading opposition politician] who said that Martin Luther King Jr. had a list of over a hundred means of civil disobedience."

was clear. Marcos might still be in town but he was no longer President. We had only one and that was President Aquino. I had written "President Aquino" in all correspondence since February 15, but saying it out loud in public was a big breakthrough and my voice broke a little. I tried to outline to the group what seemed to be the current situation. "There are only two alternatives: either we stay put here until things are clearer, or we show our solidarity with the reformists and march somewhere—to Malacañang,[3] to Channel 4, to EDSA."

The group decided to go to EDSA. I warned the kids. "This is a revolution, please do not expect a picnic. We must be prepared for everything. There are no casualties yet because they do not shoot face to face, but behind big tanks, from the air, everything becomes impersonal." Then rally-hardened youth took over, naming defense units, marshals, negotiating panel. While I privately debated if I would go, having promised Ben to stay put in the office, the choice was made for me when they asked me to be with the nego[tiating] panel. . . . I also felt I would never be able to forgive myself if anything happened to those kids in my absence. . . .

We walked swiftly, punctuating the air with "Marcos, Marcos *mandaraya*" (Marcos, cheater, to the tune of the Battle Hymn of the Republic) and other chants. All the way, people came out to meet us, hands raised in the *Laban* (Fight!) sign, some joining in the chants. It suddenly reminded me of what is probably my first memory, American GIs marching to the friendly wave of the populace during what is still "The Liberation" in our history books. I was three at the time of the end of World War II. I stopped the memories with louder chants, unwilling now to attach that or any other liberation to a foreign power.

And then we got to EDSA and found what we had not expected: THE REVOLUTION WAS A PICNIC!!! Banners of different colors (mostly yellow, some Salvador Laurel's green, some Communist red, the Philippine flag), ingenious placards and posters, . . . the informal economy in full bloom—corn (yellow[4] of course), peanuts, drinks (but not the boycotted San Miguel products), political items—"Cory is our President" fans, sponge hands in the Laban sign, yellow ribbons. There were choirs and street theater, mini-rallies, people eating, sleeping, milling around. Civilians—including many children—crowded the raised sen-

---

[3] *Malacañang*: the presidential palace.
[4] Yellow was the color of Cory Aquino's presidential campaign.

try houses at Aguinaldo,[5] its main gate proclaiming whom they recognized as President. Images of Virgin Mary and the Sto. Niño [the Holy Infant] were everywhere. Nevertheless, at the edges remained the tanks and near the Logistics Command, marines with fixed eyes and bayonets, oblivious of the people, waiting for the order to attack.

What kinds of people were there? Priests and nuns were conspicuous in their *sotanas* and *habitos* [cassocks and habits], so were Americans with cameras. There were recognizable organizations, hastily formed groups and three-generation families. There were delegations from Southern Tagalog and Central Luzon, some even as far as . . . Antique. . . . I saw a neighbor with *balikbayan* (Filipinos based abroad visiting the country) relatives in tow, friends I have not seen for many years, my son's buddies from the Ellinwood Youth Choir. . . . If one could tell class from clothes and bearing, I think the congregation represented the entire class structure. Later, one of my students would talk of co-rallyists who walked all the way from and to Baclaran (20 kilometers each way) because they did not have the bus fare. . . .

Three friends and I joined the people escorting soldiers who had been talked into joining Enrile and Ramos. We waved at them and they waved back, putting their armalites [assault rifles] aloft. Earlier, someone cautioned June Keithley that Ramos should confiscate all arms of the surrenderees. Sensible advice in normal times. But here they were, walking single file, happy, flashing their weapons while people showered them with cigarettes, gave food, offered drink and drowned them with shouts of "Cory, Cory." They were followed by their truck now filled with civilians singing and shouting, "To Ramos we go." My hair stood on end; this is a revolution?

As we walked on a slope in EDSA, its rolling nature unnoticed with[out] the packed traffic it usually holds, we saw people still coming, in buses and cars, on jeeps, on foot, mothers carrying babies, as far as the eye could see. . . . It was a mass of humanity that poured out to show Marcos that he does not cow anyone anymore. Marcos would stay on until Tuesday evening, but by Monday night, he was simply a hated irrelevance. He still had weapons . . . ; he could still kill and maim a few of us, but unless he dropped an atomic bomb, he could not destroy all the waves of people that would brandish the rosary and their bodies as their only weapons. He imposed a curfew of 6 p.m. while hundreds of thousands remained in the streets and stayed

---

[5]*Aguinaldo*: Camp Aguinaldo, headquarters of the Armed Forces of the Philippines.

beneath the stars at EDSA, the television channels, Malacañang, all through the night. No one enforced his order. . . .

Tuesday. Gabby called up around 7 a.m. saying that our group would start to march at 8. I told him not to wait for me. I would return to the barricades, but only with my family. I did not want my children to miss this chance of defending the army. (Later, Andy would comment: "Didn't you realize that if the soldiers shot, your entire family would have been decimated?" . . . I did not think of that. I was more afraid that my children would say to their grandchildren that the revolution passed them by because their parents did not let them join it. Telling posterity I had the chance and did not become involved was for me the greater risk and shame. . . .)

The children and I convinced their father that they should join the barricades. We decided to go in the evening, so we could stay as long as we wanted. . . . After a circuitous route, we finally got to the Ortigas-EDSA area. The big surprise was not the crowd, which we expected, but how easy it was to negotiate in it, how vast the reservoir of goodwill people displayed. These were not the usual demons of the streets that make Manila traffic a nightmare. Even parking was a cinch. We created a rudimentary organization, appointing Leo (my sister's husband) at our head and telling the teenagers they were not to overtake him. Then we took off, leaving in the cars most of the provisions we brought along. (I had food and wet towels in case of tear gas; they always tried to attack at night.) . . . I pointed out to my kids the railing on the islands and the huge rocks from a construction site that people had moved to block the loyalist troops from EDSA. Then we walked toward the camps, giving way to a group of men in wheelchairs who were also volunteer defenders. . . .

About 30 minutes into our march, I suggested stopping to really listen to the radio. And there it was: another unconfirmed report that the Marcoses had fled to Clark Air Force Base,[6] by helicopter or land convoy it was not clear. . . . We sat on the sidewalk, excitement rising. Still no confirmation, but people had started to enter Malacañang. General Ramos went on the air to warn against looting, to remind the people that although the objects there might seem frivolous and extravagant, they were now public property and should be protected. This was no false alarm. But the news would not be confirmed until the morning.

---

[6] *Clark Air Force Base*: a U.S. base deactivated in 1991.

Was it a glorious moment? There on the sidewalk, eating peanuts, we believed the unconfirmed report and then decided to go home.... All through the ride home, we tooted our horn, Cory, Cory. Strangers all, we flashed the L and said Mabuhay.[7] ... We saw soldiers walking home to Fort Bonifacio, a makeshift Cory banner as their protection. We "coryed" to them and they shyly raised their Ls to us. If the citizens did not harm those who were poised to kill them, why would we harm these poor draftees? "*Tapos na,*" we shouted. ("It's all over.") They raised their Ls again.

Hiyas fell asleep on my lap, her fingers still showing the L, and she would hold her hand high each time another car greeted us first, automatically, as in a dream. I kissed her head and said softly to the child I bore after three months of martial law, "Finally *anak* (Daughter), you can breathe the air of freedom." She got up with a start, exulting, "Oh, yes, oh yes. *Kuya* (Older Brother), you had two years over me, is the air better now?" She would not forget that moment of realization. Then Ben said, "Anak, just don't forget. Never again a Marcos." No, we did not dance in the streets. But we made a pledge. Never again a dictator. We know our power now. Let Cory and her successors watch out.

---

[7] *Mabuhay:* a common celebratory greeting roughly equivalent to "Viva!"

4

Chile, 1982–1988

In broad outlines, the Chilean case follows the scenario seen in the Philippines: A repressive dictatorship is installed and maintained with U.S. economic and military support but begins to weaken in the early 1980s as an economic downturn makes the regime's excesses harder to tolerate. In the middle of the decade, a Communist insurgency loses its potency while U.S. support for the dictator is (reluctantly) tempered. Finally, the dictator stages an election he believes he cannot lose, only to discover that a half-decade of social mobilization, with the Catholic Church actively involved and the political opposition increasingly committed to nonviolence, means that the people are more willing to risk dissent than anyone expected. The dictator is humiliated.

There are also significant differences with the Philippine case. While the U.S. presence in the Western Pacific from the 1960s was anchored in the geopolitics of the cold war, Latin America was perceived, by U.S. leaders, as their backyard. The needs of multinational corporations, such as copper mining interests in Chile, shaped U.S. relations with Latin America as much as did fears of the spread of communism.

For Chileans, September 11 will always signify the day in 1973 that General Augusto Pinochet led a coup d'état (with U.S. support) that toppled the democratically elected government of President Salvador Allende, a Socialist. Pinochet promised to restore order and bring economic prosperity. He succeeded in the latter for a while, as the Chilean economy expanded greatly through the 1970s. Whether Pinochet established order depended on one's perspective, because his regime arrested, tortured, and killed thousands of opponents across the country. In the process, most political parties and social organizations were forced out of existence or underground.

The coup provoked deep tactical conflicts within the major parties. Some Christian Democratic leaders accepted the coup, whereas others were more concerned about the destruction of democracy. Socialist leaders in exile and in the underground debated whether armed revolution (inspired by Cuba, in particular) was the way to liberate Chile. However, with normal politics severely restricted by Pinochet, opposition politicians became ever more isolated from the people of Chile. Indeed, Pinochet seemed invincible for much of his first decade in power. But when the economy nosedived in 1982, protest began to swell. Copper miners called a national strike in May 1983, and students at university campuses across the country followed suit with months of raucous demonstrations. The question for Chilean politicians was what value the protests had. Were the students and workers Marxists who should be shunned, or were they potential allies in the fight for democracy?

Where normal politics withered, social movements stepped into the breach. These were of three overlapping kinds. Some dissidents searched for a way to publicize the disappearances of so many Chileans. Drawing in part on a strong feminist movement (see Document 5), women—especially the mothers and wives of those who disappeared—began to organize. Women's protests often articulated what others feared to express, and sometimes the regime did not retaliate. The founders of Women for Life (Mujeres por la Vida), for example, denounced the government's "system of death" at the group's founding press conference in November 1983, promising to defend the lives of their children; some ten thousand women attended their first action a month later.[1] Other opposition arose in the Catholic Church (Document 18). As in the other country cases so far examined, the Church remained an institution that the regime could not touch. At the same time, high unemployment and poverty under Pinochet kept left-wing political groups strong in the shantytowns (*poblaciones*), where guerrilla theater thrived (Document 17).

The Christian Democratic Party and the Catholic Church, led by Archbishop Juan Fresno, began talking with moderate Socialists. They found common ground in an acceptance of nonviolence and formed the Democratic Alliance. In August 1985, parties in the Alliance reached agreement on what they called the National Accord for Transition to Full Democracy, urging an end to the nearly constant states of emergency and substantial changes to the constitution. The National Accord (to which Gabriel Valdés refers in Document 19) did not bring about political change, but for the first time there was a concrete political platform offering a nonviolent alternative to Pinochet.

---

[1]A parallel movement emerged in Argentina, where the Mothers of the Plaza de Mayo staged weekly marches from 1977. See Temma Kaplan, *Taking Back the Streets: Women, Youth, and Direct Democracy* (Berkeley: University of California Press, 2003).

But finding a middle ground was not easy. To the right, conservative parties knew that however much they had lost faith in Pinochet, his rule had ended the anarchy they associated with the Allende government. To the left, the Communists continued to wage campaigns of sabotage and guerrilla violence, aiming to make Chile ungovernable. In September 1986, they staged an assassination attempt on Pinochet's motorcade; a rocket launcher attack killed five of his bodyguards but left Pinochet virtually unscathed.

This attack was ironically the breakthrough Chile needed, but not in the way the Communists expected. Rather than being inspired by the audacity of the attack, the Chilean public was repulsed. Meanwhile, Pinochet seized the opportunity to crack down with renewed intensity. Now feeling invincible, he went ahead with plans for the presidential plebiscite promised in 1980—with himself (and not, for example, some trusted civilian conservative) as the only candidate. The majority of Chileans, he felt sure, would choose him over uncertainty and disorder. The fate of Ferdinand Marcos had made an impression on Pinochet and his advisers; they resolved that this election would be clean. Some opposition parties were allowed to register and campaign for a "No" vote in the plebiscite and even to run daily advertisements on television.

The "No" campaign's victory in the plebiscite on October 5, 1988, may now seem preordained, but it appeared as unlikely beforehand as opposition victories in Poland and the Philippines did. The main obstacle was the understandable reluctance of Chileans to engage in a process that might be both dangerous and futile. Just as in the other cases, however, years of protest and grassroots organization broke down people's reluctance to be involved while also giving activists the training they needed to engage in a massive propaganda campaign. Nearly 55 percent of the electorate rejected Pinochet.

The "No" victory was the culminating moment of the Chilean revolution. The process would take another year, during which Pinochet reluctantly agreed to major reforms, and both sides prepared for parliamentary and (real) presidential elections in December 1989. The opposition's candidate, Christian Democrat Patricio Aylwin, defeated the new conservative standard bearer, young finance minister Hernán Büchi. The political transformation of Chile showed that even a relatively prosperous dictatorship could lose its reason for existence as the cold war unwound. The balance in Latin America now shifted decisively in favor of democracy.

In reading these documents, consider how the forms of protest might be shaped by the fact that repression in Chile was much more deadly than in Poland. A comparison with the Philippine case is also instructive: Both protest movements culminated in a national vote, but how did opposition strategies differ, and why? Would the concept of patriotic realism (Document 19) have made sense to Filipino or Polish protesters?

17

LOS DE ALVEAR

The Contest

1982

How could an opposition reach people who normally did not engage in politics? This document, a political skit, and the next one offer examples. The Contest can be contrasted with the Orange Alternative's "happenings" in Poland. In both Chile and Poland, humor could offer an antidote to despair and perhaps an invitation to participation; in Chile, however, the information about economic theories and U.S. complicity in Chilean hardship was as important as the entertainment itself.

Los de Alvear—the name possibly referring to Bishop Enrique Alvear of Pudahuel, Santiago, who worked actively among the poor—was one of many theater collectives that emerged in the poblaciones *of Santiago and other cities in the late 1970s, formed by local members of the Communist party or of one of the many splinters of the Socialist party. These collectives wrote and performed their skits in factories, churches, and homes to raise consciousness and draw others into political activism. The skits employed broad humor and pop-culture references. Some portrayed the family dramas in working-class settings;* The Contest *is easier to recognize as part of the story of Chilean opposition because it seeks to relate everyday problems to the national and international situation. The reader should imagine it as broad farce, with comic accents, music, and props.*

From Grupo Los de Alvear, "El concurso," in *Poética de la población marginal. Teatro Poblacional Chileno: 1978–1985—Antología Crítica*, ed. Diego Muñoz, Carlos Oschsenius, José Luis Olivari, and Hernán Vidal (Minneapolis: Prisma Institute, 1987), 205–11. Translated by José Najar.

CHARACTERS:

The Host
Mr. Ronaldo Frioman[1]
Members of the Jury: LAMPARITO
JAMONES *(wearing a low-cut
flowery dress, and speaking in
an Afro-Caribbean accent)*;

GUALO REYES;[2] RAFAELA
GARRAFA[3]
MISS LIBERTAD MERCADO [Miss
Free Market]
MISS JUSTINA SOLIDARIA [Miss
Justice Solidarity]
JUANITO CESANTÍA [Johnny
Unemployment]

*(The play begins with the music of a large orchestra; the Host enters
smiling, wearing a formal suit.)*

HOST: Ladies and gentlemen, Good evening. We are happy to be here
once again with you and with all of our TV viewers. We are sure
you are as eager as we are to finally discover who will be elected
Miss Economy 1982. We have selected two beautiful finalists who
are fighting tooth and nail for the crown. But first, I am pleased to
introduce to you the personalities who make up our wonderful jury.
I have the honor now to present to you the president of the jury,
Mr. Ronaldo Frioman!

*(Cowboy music plays as Mr. Frioman appears, dressed in a cowboy hat,
flowered print shirt, white pants, and sunglasses, with a cigar in his
mouth and a camera slung over his shoulder. He strides to the micro-
phone.)*

MR. FRIOMAN: Me feel very happy to be in Chili, ai lav yu, ai uant yu,
ai ni yu.

HOST: What a charming man, people! Let's hear a round of applause
for the gentleman.

[Next, the Host introduces the members of the jury one by one.] . . .

HOST: OK, ladies and gentlemen, the time has come to present the
finalists of this great contest, to choose Miss Economy. First, let's
welcome Ms. Libertad Mercado to the stage.

---

[1] *Frio* means "cold." This is a reference both to Ronald Reagan and to his economic
adviser, Milton Friedman.
[2] In name, dress, and character, Gualo Reyes is supposed to represent the average
Chilean guy.
[3] Her name evokes Raffaella Carrà, an Italian singer popular at the time in Latin
America. She represents foreigners, especially Europeans, who do not understand Chile
very well.

(Miss Mercado comes out; the Host offers his arm to her. She looks at him carefully and accepts. They walk around the stage and stop by the jury table. The music being played is in English.)

HOST: Next, ladies and gentlemen, let me introduce the second finalist, Miss . . . Justina Solidaria!

(A young girl appears on stage, seeming a bit shy. Suddenly, the Host remembers that he has to offer his arm to her and does so. Folk music accompanies their walk around the stage. She stands next to Miss Mercado, who looks at her with disdain.)

HOST: Well, the time has come to ask the three rigorous questions to the contestants. The first one goes to Miss Mercado, and it is asked by Mr. Frioman.

MR. FRIOMAN: What do you do to look in such good shape?

LIBERTAD: Well, you know . . . I have never told anyone, but today I will reveal my secret: I used to follow the "moon diet,"[4] but nine years ago,[5] more or less, I came across a better one and I have never felt better than with my current diet.

HOST: How nice! A round of applause, ladies and gentlemen. Let's hear now the question for Miss Solidaria. Lamparito Jamones will ask the question.

(Justina steps forward.)

LAMPARITO: Tell me dear, what do you do to look the way you do? But really tell me, sugar!

JUSTINA: Well, I used to be a strong and healthy little girl; I was growing stronger among my people without any problems; but one day my parents became neglectful and I, without knowing what I was doing, took a glass that was sitting on the kitchen table and I drank it all, and ever since I have had indigestion. I still have not recovered.

HOST: I think we all want to know what you drank.

JUSTINA: It was Gorilla's milk.[6]

---

[4] *"moon diet"*: a fasting, month-long cyclical diet popular at the time.

[5] "Nine years" refers to the 1973 coup by Pinochet. The audience would associate Pinochet's regime with the imposition of economic restrictions.

[6] *Gorilla*: a slang term for military officer. This is another reference to the 1973 military coup.

HOST: You have heard the contestant's answer, but let's not become too sad. Tonight is a night of happiness. Let's hear Miss Mercado's second question. This one will be asked by Gualo Reyes.

GUALO: What message would you give to all youth that admires you?

LIBERTAD: I would tell them that the main thing is to fight to achieve success in life, because this is how one can help in the formation of a great country, stronger and more sovereign. Therefore youth must strive to achieve success so that we can buy televisions, cars, houses, telephones, etc. Everything one wants. But I will repeat: get to the top regardless of who falls. Long live my country, and long live the unity of youth![7]

HOST: How nice! Let's give her a round of applause, ladies and gentlemen. What intelligence! Let's hear the second question for Miss Justina. This one will be asked by the incomparable Rafaela.

RAFAELA: I would like to ask, what message would you give the youth?

JUSTINA: For them to take good care of themselves, especially when they are growing up because if they don't, they might end up with one of the epidemics that we have around here: consumerism, selfishness, etc. In any case, I will give you a recipe to heal yourselves: hot water, herb of solidarity and a little branch of justice. This needs to be sweetened with love. This is a recipe that I learned from my people.

HOST: You have heard the contestant's second answer. Let's hear now the last question for Miss Mercado. This one will be asked by the president of the jury.

MR. FRIOMAN: What are you planning to do with your future?

LIBERTAD: I hope to find a millionaire economist to keep me well off ... with a house, a car ... everything I desire. I would like to have three children with him. Because I am well-planned, I even have their names. The first I would call SUCCESS, the second one CONSUME and the third one INTEREST.

HOST: How nice! Let's give Miss Mercado a round of applause. There is a reason why she made it to the finals! To finish up with the questions, the last one will be for Miss Justina and I will ask it myself. What are you planning to do with your future?

---

[7]Here she imitates a political slogan.

JUSTINA: I am thinking of going back to my people to see if they will give me the cure I need to recover once and for all, and if I win, I will win for everyone. I will always be with the people because I don't want anything for myself. Thank you.

HOST: Good, now the contestants have answered their three questions, and we hope the jury is now ready to deliberate. While they do that, we will go to a commercial break and we will be right back.

(The Host and the contestants exit, the jury begins to deliberate, speaking all at once, until Mr. Frioman interrupts.)

MR. FRIOMAN: No, no, no, me don't like to argue very much, that is why me say me don't like Justina, but Libertad Mercado is *mucho bueno* with her two interest rates and her capital fund appearing very liquefiable. Me vote for her.

LAMPARITO: Hey, watch out, you're pressuring us, that's what I think. Come on, dude.

GUALO: For sure, I like Justina. She is so little and so charming, I feel very sorry for what happened to her as a child. As soon as I see her, I will invite her over to my home.

RAFAELA: I think that the best *bambina* is Miss Mercado. She has *molto* going for her. She is attractive and has a great presence.

MR. FRIOMAN: Look, I am telling you that we need to elect Miss Mercado, because then we will help this country become famous for having elected this Miss Economía. Lots of tourists will come, investors, capitalists, lenders. . . . That's why I am asking you with much love that we all vote for Miss Marketing *[in English in the original]*.

LAMPARITO: I can't believe this, I can't believe this! You are more hateful than Soleá's son.[8] You are pressuring us, you really pressure us.

GUALO: I'll vote, because I have to. I like Justina, but I must swallow my tears, and vote for Mercado. Ciao pals.

RAFAELA: I vote for Mercado because she has so much, so much more.

---

[8] *Soleá*: a shortened form of Soledad, who was the title character, cursed with ungrateful sons, of a Mexican telenovela (soap opera) that was immensely popular in Chile in 1982.

MR. FRIOMAN: It has been decided, Miss Liberty Marketing is elected Miss Economía, because Miss Justina is too ordinary. . . . She goes with everyone, she would not be a good queen.

(The Host walks onto the stage while Mr. Frioman fans himself with some dollars as he smiles.)

HOST: Well, ladies and gentlemen. How wonderful! We finally have a decision from the jury. Let's bring back the contestants! *(The contestants come back, Libertad looking proud and Justina looking humble. The Host takes an envelope from the jury's president.)* Ladies and gentlemen . . . we have finally a decision from the jury. I will open the envelope containing the name of Miss Economía 1982. It is Miss . . .

(Suddenly a child appears, running toward Miss Libertad Mercado, who is scared and ashamed. The child is ragged and filthy. A banner on his chest reads: SCARCITY/HIGH PRICES.)

CESANTÍA: Mom! Mommy! My little brother Recession fell over and broke his nose. He tripped over the plan, the economic plan.

(A great disturbance erupts; everyone talks at once. Libertad takes the child by the arm and leaves very quickly. The Host holds his head in his hands, while the members of the jury exit. Finally he is alone.)

HOST: Such problems happen even in the best of contests. I beg your understanding of Miss Mercado. It is the bad examples that come from the outside. I have one last message for you: although I have not identified myself, I will take serious measures to reactivate the controls of the Miss Economía contest. . . .

(While music plays, the Host leaves the stage dancing.)

THE END

18

SEBASTIÁN ACEVEDO MOVEMENT AGAINST TORTURE

Protest against El Mercurio
November 21, 1983

Sebastián Acevedo was an ordinary worker in the city of Concepción whose teenage children, suspected of subversive activity, disappeared after being detained by the police. Driven to despair by his inability to find them, Acevedo set himself on fire outside the city's cathedral on November 11, 1983. His death galvanized Catholic activists who had been trying to draw attention to the human rights abuses of the Pinochet regime. Father Jose Aldunate had begun leading street protests in front of police stations and other known incarceration sites; in these demonstrations, a small group of people unfurled banners saying "People Are Tortured Here" and sang in hopes that those imprisoned might hear. Torture facilities were generally unmarked, and the courts and newspapers kept silent; thus public witness was an essential weapon that made the unspeakable known. Aldunate's group adopted Acevedo's name.

Just ten days after Acevedo's death, some three hundred people—including priests and nuns but also lay human rights activists and others—gathered in front of the offices of El Mercurio, *a Santiago daily paper seen as a mouthpiece of the Pinochet regime. The Acevedo Movement staged nearly two hundred such protests; each was scripted with songs and a litany, a petition delivered in a call-and-response format. In this way, even casual participants had something concrete to do. Some of them would warm to the rhythms reminiscent of a folk concert; others would find comfort in the rituals of a Catholic Mass.*

SONG: "I INVOKE YOU, LIBERTY."

For the caged bird
For the fish in the fish tank

Hernán Vidal, *El Movimiento Contra la Tortura 'Sebastián Acevedo': Derechos Humanos y la Producción de Símbolos Nacionales bajo el Fascismo Chileno* (Minneapolis: Institute for the Study of Ideologies and Literature, 1986), 332–35, 340–41. Translated by José Najar.

For my friend that is in jail
For saying what was on his mind
For the wrenched flowers
For the trampled-on grass
For the pruned trees
For the tortured bodies
I invoke you, liberty.

For the persecuted ideas
For the beatings received
For that one who does not resist
For those who hide
For the fear they have of you
For your steps they keep watch for
For the way they attack you
For the children whom they are killing
I invoke you, liberty.

I name you in the name of everyone
By your real name
I name you at dusk
When no one sees you.
I write your name
On the walls of my city (repeat).

For the clenched teeth
For the suppressed fury
For the lump in one's throat
For the mouths that do not sing
For the clandestine kiss
For the censured verse
For the youth in exile
For the prohibited names
I invoke you, liberty.

For the invaded lands
For the conquered peoples
For the subjugated people
For the exploited men
For the deaths at the stake
For the righteous who are condemned

For the assassinated hero
For the extinguished fires
I invoke you, liberty.

I invoke you in the name of everyone . . .

PUBLIC DENUNCIATION

Look! Some will read the entire phrase, and ALL will repeat [the bold phrase] very slow and very loud.
A father has immolated himself
so that the CNI[1] **return to him his children.**
The news hits around the world but the national press conceals it, **El Mercurio hides it.**
For 10 years in Chile **a servile press has stayed silent.**
We denounce this press. . . .
This press keeps silence about torture and thus **becomes a torturer itself,**
keeps silent about the disappeared and thus **it also disappears people,**
keeps silent about the secret prisons and thus **it keeps them in custody,**
cowardly keeps silent about what the CNI says and does, and thus **collaborates with the CNI.**
We call on El Mercurio and **the entire national press**
to launch a campaign **against torture, against secret prisons, for the abolishing and dismantling of the CNI.**
If they do not do it, to cease once and for all **to utter any word of any value,**
to provide any constructive contribution[2]
to the building of a democracy and **a future for Chile.**

LITANY

Those who are at the front	*Those who are in the back*
Of the death of Víctor Jara[3] . . .	El Mercurio is an accomplice

[1] *CNI*: Centro Nacional de Informaciones (National Information Center), the Chilean secret police.

[2] *El Mercurio* often seemed to straddle the issues; here the Acevedo Movement calls on *El Mercurio* to take a stand, one way or the other.

[3] *Víctor Jara* (1932–1973): a popular folk singer who was arrested and killed just days after Pinochet seized power.

of the sacrifice of José Tohá[4] ...

El Mercurio is an accomplice

of the torture and assassination
of María Ugarte ...

El Mercurio is an accomplice

of the disappearance of Carlos
Lorca and so many others ...

El Mercurio is an accomplice

of the massacre of peasants
from Lonquén ...

El Mercurio is an accomplice

of the assassinations in Laja ...

El Mercurio is an accomplice

of the clandestine burials in
Mulchén ...

El Mercurio is an accomplice

of the torture until death of
Eduardo Jara ...

El Mercurio is an accomplice

of the blows that killed
Professor Alvarez ...

El Mercurio is an accomplice

of the bullets that assassinated
Hugo Rivero ...

El Mercurio is an accomplice

of the butchery practiced on
the person of D. Huerta

El Mercurio is an accomplice

of the techniques of torture
practiced on fired unionists ...

El Mercurio is an accomplice

of the massacres of August and
September committed by the
Carabineros ...

El Mercurio is an accomplice

of the secret prison on
Havana Street in Valparaíso ...

El Mercurio is an accomplice

of the persecution of the leaders
of the 8th Region ...

El Mercurio is an accomplice

of the torture of the children of
Sebastián Acevedo ...

El Mercurio is an accomplice

of the permanent mistreatment of
political prisoners ...

El Mercurio is an accomplice

of the moral torture of those
in exile ...

El Mercurio is an accomplice

of the silence regarding the fate
of the disappeared ...

El Mercurio is an accomplice

of the immorality of the
auto-amnesty of 1978[5] ...

El Mercurio is an accomplice

---

[4]*José Tohá* (1927–1974): a Socialist politician and journalist. Subsequent references in this litany are to a mixture of well-known and local victims of Pinochet's regime.

[5]*auto-amnesty of 1978*: a decree by Pinochet granting amnesty to the military for all crimes since September 1973.

DIALOG (very slow and very loud)

Look! Questions: Those in front   *Answers: Those in the back*

—Can an accomplice to torture
speak of humanity?   —No, he cannot
—Can an accomplice to
torture speak of democracy?   —No, he cannot
—Can an accomplice to torture
speak of coexistence?   —No, he cannot
—Can an accomplice to torture
speak of peace?   —No, he cannot
—Can an accomplice to torture
speak of the common good?   —No, he cannot
—Can an accomplice to torture
speak of liberty?   —No, he cannot
—Can an accomplice to
torture speak of honor?   —No, he cannot
—Can an accomplice to torture
speak of honesty?   —No, he cannot
—Can an accomplice to torture
speak of truth?   —No, he cannot
—Can an accomplice to torture
speak of awareness?   —No, he cannot
—Can an accomplice to torture
speak of justice?   —No, he cannot
—Can an accomplice to torture
lecture on Christian conduct?   —No, he cannot
—Can an accomplice to torture
lecture on human rights?   —No, he cannot
—Can an accomplice to torture
lecture on violence and nonviolence?   —No, he cannot
—Can an accomplice to torture
lecture on political ethics?   —No, he cannot
—Can an accomplice to torture
lecture on Western and Christian
civilization?   —No, he cannot

SONG [REPEAT "I INVOKE YOU, LIBERTY"]

19

GABRIEL VALDÉS

Speech at Democratic Alliance Rally
November 21, 1985

The rally in support of the National Accord for Transition to Full Democracy marked the return of Chilean society to the public sphere. It was not angry students or workers who marched in the streets, but rather a half-million people gathered in O'Higgins Park, Santiago, under the banners of various parties from the center and left. They hailed not only from the Democratic Alliance, which had called the rally, but also from the Communist-allied Popular Democratic Movement. Permission to hold the rally was about the only thing that Alliance leaders like Gabriel Valdés (1919–) won from Pinochet at this time. Nonetheless, the rally did demonstrate quite graphically that the political divisions that had weakened the opposition for so long were themselves weakening. Valdés's chief goals in this address were to provide a platform of unity with which all in his audience could identify and to outline a program of what he calls "patriotic realism."

Chilean Men and Women,
Who are we?
Who are we who are gathered here?
This vast multitude represents the Chilean people, the women and
   men of the Republic's capital. . . .

In these twelve years of dictatorship, the government has replicated nature: earthquakes of violence of armed men against unarmed men; a flood of foreign products, tsunamis of repression. The Chileans have lived isolated, fearfully waiting for eruptions of bad temper, for the spirit of vengeance, the fiery lava of repression, or the ashes of useless words.

From "El discurso de Valdés: Presidente del PDC habló a nombre de la Alianza para exegir 'el mínimo de buena fe requerido,'" *Hoy* (Santiago), 436, November 25–December 1, 1985, 11–13. Translated by José Najar.

We, the Chileans, have always been a people who have suffered in the face of nature's misfortunes. But none of us is going to tolerate the dictatorship as a necessary misfortune. . . . For a number of years we have been fighting for freedom. Any spaces [for freedom] that we have, we have won by acts of sacrifice and democratic faith. . . . Thanks to the generous patriotism of the Cardinal Archbishop of Santiago, Monsignor Fresno, the National Accord for the Transition to Full Democracy was created. These are fundamental steps to realize the will of civil society. We are in a hurry now because each minute longer of the dictatorship will weigh an hour in the future democracy. . . .

A few days ago . . . Cardinal Fresno, in a profound meditation on power said: "There are some people who believe they have power over men because they have in their hands instruments of death and domination. There are some who believe that their power is imperishable and behave like gods putting themselves above other men with pride and arrogance." Here lies the most powerful source of violence. That is why we say that Mr. Pinochet is not the son of Chile's Republican culture.

In Chile there will never be democracy if the culture of violence persists! In Chile there will never be democracy if we do not replace the rifle with the vote! In Chile there will never be the desired peace if there is no end to cowardly and anonymous terrorism! No Chilean can be another Chilean's Cain! There is no moral justification for murder, or to unleash revenge instincts. We do not want a Homeland where one pays an eye for an eye, a tooth for a tooth. . . .

On behalf of the political parties and social movements of the Democratic Alliance, I beg of Chileans, I implore Chileans to put an end to the culture of death. Put an end to terrorism. For peace to come about, without which Chile's history will be futile. . . . If there are no channels of free expression the desperate will explode, or those who believe that death is an argument to persuade will gain. Once again, here and now, we denounce this monstrous dialectic. We demand democracy because we want to live worthwhile lives. . . .

In a democracy we can avoid the blood and the tears! But nobody should cultivate the illusion of ending all shared sweat and sacrifice. Mr. General, we are responsible politicians and we do not encourage easy ways out or illusions. You, Sir, are the great demagogue: you promised cars, televisions and phones to almost all Chilean families. . . .

We are here to start the final phase of this great civic struggle. We are here to demand democracy. We believe that the National Accord is a civilized instrument to achieve democracy. We must sustain and deepen it because it contains the essential foundations for a civilized life. If some consider it insufficient we call on their patriotic realism: acknowledge that the National Accord is a just and serious proposal. . . . Without the National Accord, we would be heading towards a Civil War!

For those who do not understand this dramatic hour for Chile, enough with the hesitations and fears. The time has come to decide between dictatorship and the building of a responsible democracy.

To begin, we demand immediate compliance with the measures envisaged in the National Accord. . . .

We demand the full restoration of workers' rights; . . .

We demand the full restoration of civil liberties;

We demand the return of citizenship to those who were deprived of it;

We demand the end to the suspension of political rights and the abrogation of restrictive rules;

We demand full respect for human rights. . . .

We want a democracy based on justice, whose ethical foundation is full respect for human rights; which will recognize those institutions that ensure the fullest development of individual freedoms, and institutions that safeguard the rights of us all. . . .

Once again, I reiterate that democracy will not be easy. We cannot expect anything but sacrifice that is long and sustained, collective, and national. Nothing will be accomplished easily at the beginning, but with the Accord, we will begin to recover our dignity as citizens and, most fundamentally, our liberty. . . .

If Argentina has succeeded in establishing an exemplary democracy, if Uruguay lives in democracy after years of violence, if Brazil has managed to find freedom, why can't Chile? Chile must return to the democratic community in Latin America and regain its leading role in the history of the continent.

Democracy will be the ongoing exercise of agreements and not of exclusions; of understandings and dialogues, and not of threats. . . . Democracy requires loyalty of conduct from rulers and opponents. Democracy requires an ethical basis. . . . But democracy must contain clear limits on disagreements. The rules of coexistence, the rights of citizens will necessarily have to link with the priority goals of eliminating the scandal of extreme poverty and marginalization, creating stable employment and achieving high and sustained growth rates. These are the objectives of the National Accord. These goals are difficult but not impossible. They are indispensable but we will achieve them as we achieved our independence.

We will begin to work with what we have, to live with what we have, with austerity and without ostentation, in a Chileanness, cheerful and self-confident.

Democracy is not born by concession. Just as today we have won the right to meet in this vast assembly of the people, this council [of the nation], starting today, in every city and every village, we will congregate to exercise this fundamental right. This is the oath of those of us who are here and the millions who are listening on the radio.

Women and men of Chile:

Democracy is born when a crowd becomes an organized people. And an organized people expresses itself freely in the act of perfect sovereignty. And that act is the vote. The people rise up and say "enough" to the dictatorship, to the decadence, and to the repression. The people should vote. Let no one continue to impede us from choosing our way of life and those who we choose to govern us. Let's begin a great national crusade for the right to vote. Electoral registries: yes, they were burned,[1] but they must be redone.

We want to choose, and for that we need to vote. It is the act in which the citizen, before his conscience, decides what is best for his homeland. We want to elect mayors, elect a Congress with constituent, legislatorial and fiscal capacity. We want to choose the President of the Republic.

His Holiness Pope John Paul II, through mediation, averted war with our Argentine brothers. When the Pope visits Chile[2] peace must prevail among us. Peace, whose full name is democracy. That means unity in our Chileanness. This means receiving the Pope in democracy and liberty!

Compatriots: on this afternoon all-embracing and profound, with faith, with joy, without rancor, with unshakable determination let us embark on an eternal journey that demands that we construct a democracy that will make Chile a homeland for all.

Each Chilean man and woman is an architect of peace and democracy. Everyone must conquer his or her own space of freedom. Democratic life will emerge to the extent that you live your own freedom.

The afternoon falls, let us go in peace. Let no one provoke or be provoked, let us rid ourselves of our fear of the present, because we carry in our sight the soul of the future that begins today, with the overwhelming strength of a people who have a historic mission to achieve for themselves.

[1]Chile's electoral registers were declared invalid and burned in June 1974.

[2]This visit took place in April 1987. In 1984, the pope mediated a border dispute between Argentina and Chile that had nearly led to war in the late 1970s.

20

Posters from the "No" Campaign
1988

*By the time Pinochet's plans to run for president in the October 1988 plebiscite were revealed, the nonviolent opposition of the National Accord had largely put aside political differences in favor of a united campaign against the regime. The plebiscite, in which Pinochet was the only candidate, posed a great obstacle to political mobilization, however, as most Chileans assumed that the vote would be rigged and feared the consequences of daring to reveal their preference. An even deeper problem was the nature of the plebiscite: A "Yes" vote (for Pinochet) was for order and perhaps for prosperity, as the economy had begun to revive; a "No" vote (rejecting Pinochet) offered no positive alternative. Yet Pinochet helped the opposition by basing the campaign for "Yes" on fear; thus "Yes" became negative. By contrast, the "No" Alliance (*Concertacion por el No*), headed by Christian Democrat Patricio Aylwin, presented a campaign of popular, future-oriented empowerment, as the leaflets in this selection show.*

In imagery, in argument, and in the way they addressed their audience, these posters differed sharply from the language of the regime. Instead, they resembled the messages of opposition to other dictatorships, such as those in Poland and the Philippines. The access to television and newspapers that Pinochet grudgingly allowed gave the "No" campaign unprecedented access. Intimidation from the Pinochet camp continued to the very end, but a clear majority of Chilean voters chose the "No" option. Having lost the support of his military and of the United States, Pinochet reluctantly accepted the verdict. In July 1989, a referendum on constitutional changes passed overwhelmingly, clearing the way for a real presidential election that December, in which Patricio Aylwin, candidate of the opposition coalition, handily won.

El panfleto: Plebiscito 1988 a Traves de Panfletos y Volantes, edited by Cristian Cottet Villalobos (n.p., 1988), n.p. Translated by José Najar.

"Casserole Protest."

Translation: Tuesday, August 30. All Chile says NO to Pinochet. With whistles, pots and pans, flutes, drums, and cymbals. From every home, street, and corner of Chile there will be heard a gigantic "NO TO THE TYRANT!" Get ready for the night of the 30th, and let your family, friends, and neighbors know. To victory for NO!

"To Vote NO."

Votar NO

significa que queremos participar
en la construcción de un Chile moderno,
donde las mujeres seamos valoradas
no sólo como madres y esposas
sino también como seres pensantes
que tenemos un aporte que entregar

Votemos NO
tranquilas y seguras

GANA EL NO
¡LA ALEGRIA
YA VIENE!

Sabemos
lo que queremos

¡NO!
voto de mujer

Translation: To vote NO means that we want to participate in the construction of a modern Chile, where women are valued not only as mothers and spouses, but also as thinking beings who have a contribution to make.

We will make this country spot-less!

Let us vote NO, calmly and safely.
No, the woman's vote! [on the voting booth:] Secret booth
NO is gaining! Here comes happiness!

We know what we want. NO, the woman's vote!

CHILE, LA ALEGRIA ESTA EN MARCHA!

Juntemos la alegria de norte a sur. De mar a cordillera... Todo Chile se suma a la Gran Marcha de la Alegria. La democracia viene en camino. Salgamos a recibirla en todo el país.

Concentración final en Santiago, 1º de Octubre a las 11 hrs. Panamericana Sur esq. Carlos Valdovinos.

NO

"Chile, Happiness Is on the March!"

Translation: Let us join its march, from the north to the south, from the sea to the mountains. . . . All of Chile is part of the Great March of Happiness. Democracy is on the road. Let us go out to meet it, all through the country. The Final Gathering: Santiago, October 1, at 11 a.m. Panamerican South Highway and Carlos Valdovinos Avenue.

5

South Africa, 1983–1994

The democratic revolution in South Africa has many features quite unlike those seen in the other revolutions examined in this book. First, although for most residents of the country the apartheid regime was a cruel dictatorship, for a sizable minority, including many who were not at all wealthy, it had all the trappings of democracy. Second, whereas racial or ethnic tensions were factors in many other cases (such as the Philippines and Ukraine), the oppression of blacks by whites was the heart of the South African problem. Third, opposition leaders in South Africa confronted the limits of peaceful resistance in a country whose leaders did not hesitate to kill their opponents. And finally, while charismatic leaders emerged in other revolutions, no figure reached the stature of Nelson Mandela, whose twenty-seven years in prison gave him moral authority matched at the time only by that of Pope John Paul II.

The apartheid regime, established formally in 1948, was also an expression of nationalism on the part of the Afrikaner people, who were whites descended from Dutch settlers of the seventeenth century. As such, it professed to be not a policy of discrimination but of separateness. Each racial group — blacks, Indians, "colored" or mixed-race, and whites (including English speakers) — was governed by separate laws to a degree well beyond what was the case in other segregated societies like the U.S. South. The regime created artificial "homelands," colloquially known as *bantustans*, to which it tried to restrict black South Africans according to their tribal or ethnic background; travel outside of these areas was possible only on the basis of easily rescinded passes. The culmination of this elaborate system was the creation in 1984 of three parallel parliaments for whites, Indians, and "coloreds," with the latter two having considerably less power.

This institutionalized form of racism, in a state that could draw on significant resources (a much larger European minority than in other African states, as well as extremely valuable reserves of raw materials) to maintain a modern infrastructure, made overthrow much more difficult. In the end, the regime's stability may have contributed as well to the peaceful nature of the revolution, as the apparatus of a modern industrial democracy proved amenable to an orderly transition of power once the custodians of apartheid realized they could not maintain their hold.

The chief organization opposing apartheid was the African National Congress (ANC), founded in 1912. From its beginning, the ANC espoused nonviolence, which was a central philosophy in the country where Mahatma Gandhi of India had begun his career and developed modern methods of passive resistance. Yet the brutal massacres of civilians at Sharpeville in March 1960 and of schoolchildren at Soweto in June 1976 demonstrated that this regime would not hesitate to kill. Nelson Mandela helped to form the ANC's military wing in 1961; he and other ANC leaders came to see bombings and guerrilla warfare as a necessary counterpart to the ideal of nonviolence. Violent confrontation, however, did not topple the apartheid state. Indeed, it allowed white South African leaders to claim that they were on the front lines of the cold war, under attack from Communists.

The prospect of peaceful change grew ever more distant in the 1970s. The Soweto massacre of 1976 and the well-publicized deaths of prominent anti-apartheid activists in police custody radicalized a new generation, represented by the Black Consciousness Movement. This generation saw its elders in the ANC as averse to confrontation and too willing to cooperate with white opponents of apartheid. Still, many South Africans of all races continued to draw inspiration from Nelson Mandela of the ANC, who had been imprisoned on Robben Island since 1964.

By 1983, the anti-apartheid forces were trapped. In prison, in exile, or underground, they had not lost the support of the majority of the population, but they could neither change the system nor improve people's lives. A movement called the United Democratic Front (UDF), created in that year, networked together hundreds of local civic, church, labor, and other organizations. Its aim was civil disobedience and local empowerment: rent boycotts, strikes, and the like. Whereas once the ANC had aimed to make South Africa "ungovernable" through violence, the UDF offered a new possibility focused on tactics that any individual could use.

Meanwhile, South Africa's international situation was changing. As in other cases in this book, the South African revolution was profoundly influenced by political movements elsewhere in the world. Many ANC leaders were in exile in neighboring countries; they also lobbied for support in Moscow or in London. In the 1980s, economic sanctions (mentioned by Desmond Tutu in Document 3) took center stage. Partially in response to the UDF-led resistance, a decades-old campaign to convince governments, corporations, and universities to withdraw investments from South Africa suddenly took off. The net result was billions of dollars withdrawn from the South African economy, putting it under severe pressure. Apartheid ceased to be an economically viable program.

Another international phenomenon, the weakening of Soviet communism, reverberated on both sides of the conflict, too, though this development did not doom the South African Communist party to irrelevance since it was not a Soviet puppet. For many in the regime, fear of the Communists was as great as fear of black rule; it was also a helpful tool in gaining Western acquiescence to the continuation of the apartheid system. All of these factors helped convince some leaders that it was time to seek an exit, even as some in the opposition realized that a nonviolent solution had to be found.

F. W. de Klerk (1936–) is comparable in many ways to Mikhail Gorbachev. Like the Soviet leader, he was an unquestioned proponent of the system he came to lead; like Gorbachev, too, he represented a younger, pragmatic generation, as interested in the economic health and international standing of the country as he was in ideology. And as had Gorbachev, de Klerk certainly hoped to save what he had inherited, but he ended up presiding over its demise. He was elected chairman of the ruling National Party in early 1989 and president later that year (at about the same age as Gorbachev had been in 1985). Just a few months later, on February 2, 1990, de Klerk announced the release of Nelson Mandela and the lifting of the ban on the ANC and other organizations.

In practical terms, de Klerk's move and Mandela's subsequent bold entry into national politics were the culmination of the South African revolution. Free elections were not held until April 1994, but the questions in the intervening years were rather how to manage the transfer of power from the Nationalist Party to the ANC and how apartheid would be dismantled and reckoned with. As they tackled this transformation, ANC leaders drew inspiration from the revolutions in Eastern Europe, inviting, for example, Adam Michnik and others from Poland to advise them. Two challenges were particularly difficult. First, violence between political factions in the black townships threatened to overwhelm the forces for positive change; hundreds of lives were lost in the late 1980s and early 1990s. Mandela addresses this problem in his speech in Document 24. Second, the violence of the apartheid regime made addressing its crimes particularly difficult. South Africa's Truth and Reconciliation Commission, established in 1995 and headed by Archbishop Desmond Tutu, became a model for addressing the crimes of the old regime in a nonviolent way and was one of the most important legacies of this revolution.

In reading these documents, consider these questions: What role does violence play in the arguments of each author? How do ideas about violence vary depending on the object of that violence? Compare arguments about negotiation with those in other cases: How might Adam Michnik (Document 9) or Jacek Kuroń (Document 12) respond to the arguments made by the ANC in Document 21, for example? And how might the ANC respond?

21

AFRICAN NATIONAL CONGRESS

On Negotiations

October 9, 1987

The African National Congress was the face of anti-apartheid resistance throughout the world and in South Africa. Many of its leaders, among them Nelson Mandela and Walter Sisulu, were imprisoned on Robben Island. Others, like ANC president Oliver Tambo, lived in exile, attempting to coordinate resistance to the apartheid regime from London and Lusaka, Zambia. This document was one of the first of a series of pronouncements on strategy, responding both to charges that the ANC was moving away from its commitment to armed resistance and to accusations that it aimed to annihilate South African society in the name of revolution. It refers to the Freedom Charter, a document drawn up in 1955 that proclaimed, "The People Shall Govern," and that advocated a nonracial South Africa.

From African National Congress, "On Negotiations," October 9, 1987. Available at the online archive of the African National Congress: http://www.anc.org.za/ancdocs/ pr/1980s/pr871009.html.

In the recent period, both the Pretoria[1] regime and various Western powers have been raising the issue of a negotiated resolution of the South African question. Inspired by the deep-seated desire and unwavering commitment to end the apartheid system as soon as possible and with minimum loss of life and property, the National Executive Committee met and considered this matter with all due seriousness and attention.

We are convinced that the Botha[2] regime has neither the desire nor the intention to engage in any meaningful negotiations. On the contrary, everything this regime does is directed at the destruction of the national liberation movement, the suppression of the democratic movement and the entrenchment and perpetuation of the apartheid system of White minority domination.

The racist regime has raised the issue of negotiations to achieve two major objectives. The first of these is to defuse the struggle inside our country by holding out false hopes of a just political settlement which the Pretoria regime has every intention to block. Secondly, this regime hopes to defeat the continuing campaign for comprehensive and mandatory sanctions by sending out bogus signals that it is ready to talk seriously to the genuine representatives of our people.

Fundamental to the understanding of the apartheid regime's concept of negotiations is the notion that it must impose its will on those it is talking to and force them to accept its dictates. In practice, the Botha regime is conducting a determined campaign of repression against the ANC and the mass democratic movement. This includes the assassination of leaders, mass detentions, military occupation of townships and a program of pacification carried out by the so-called Joint Management Centres.[3]

The racists are out to terrorize our people into submission, crush their democratic organizations and force us to surrender. All these efforts will fail. Rather than create a climate conducive to genuine negotiations, they will only serve further to sharpen the confrontation within our country and bring to the fore the prospect of the bloodiest conflict that our continent has ever seen.

---

[1] *Pretoria*: the administrative capital of South Africa.

[2] *P. W. (Pieter Willem) Botha* (1916–2006): prime minister of South Africa (1978–1984) and president (1984–1989).

[3] *Joint Management Centres*: a system of control instituted by the South African government in 1986. Some five hundred Joint Management Centres around the country gathered intelligence and conducted repressive measures against local activists.

Our struggle will not end until South Africa is transformed into a united, democratic and non-racial country. This is the only solution which would enable all our people, both Black and White, to live as equals in conditions of peace and prosperity. The overwhelming majority of our people accept that the Freedom Charter provides a reasonable and viable framework for the construction of a new society.

We wish here to reiterate that the ANC has never been opposed to a negotiated settlement of the South African question. On various occasions in the past we have, in vain, called on the apartheid regime to talk to the genuine leaders of our people. Once more, we would like to reaffirm that the ANC and the masses of our people as a whole are ready and willing to enter into genuine negotiations provided they are aimed at the transformation of our country into a united and non-racial democracy. This, and only this, should be the objective of any negotiating process. Accordingly no meaningful negotiations can take place until all those concerned, and specifically the Pretoria regime, accept this perspective which we share with the whole of humanity. . . .

We reject unequivocally the cynical demand of the Pretoria regime that we should unilaterally abandon or suspend the armed struggle. The source of violence in our country is the apartheid system. It is that violence which must end. Any cessation of hostilities would have to be negotiated and entail agreed action by both sides as part of the process of the creation of a democratic South Africa.

Equally, we reject all efforts to dictate to us who our allies should or should not be, and how our membership should be composed. Specifically, we will not bow down to pressures intended to drive a wedge between the ANC and the South African Communist Party, a tried and tested ally in the struggle for a democratic South Africa. Neither shall we submit to attempts to divide and weaken our movement by carrying out a witch hunt against various members on the basis of their ideological beliefs.

The conflict in our country is between the forces of national liberation and democracy on the one hand and those of racism and reaction on the other. Any negotiations would have to be conducted by these two forces as represented by their various organizational formations.

We reject without qualification the proposed National Council[4] which the Botha regime seeks to establish through legislation to be enacted

---

[4]Botha proposed such a council, which would include representatives of the black *bantustans*, in a speech to the new parliament in May 1987; to the ANC, it seemed to be an attempt to co-opt black leaders into a watered-down apartheid.

by the apartheid parliament. This can never be a genuine and acceptable mechanism to negotiate a democratic constitution for our country.

In practice, the National Council can never be anything more than an advisory body which would put its views to the apartheid parliament and the regime itself, which retains the right to accept or reject those views. What the Botha regime proposes as a constitution-making forum—the National Council—is therefore nothing but a device intended to enmesh all who sit on it in a bogus process of meaningless talk which has nothing to do with any genuine attempt to design a democratic constitution for our country.

In addition, this National Council seeks to entrench and legitimize the very structures of apartheid that our struggle, in all its forms, seeks to abolish. The unrepresentative organs of the apartheid structure of repression, such as the racist tricameral parliament and the *bantustans*, cannot be used as instruments for the liquidation of the very same system they have been established to maintain.

An essential part of the apartheid system is the definition and division of our people according to racial and ethnic groups, dominated by the White minority. To end apartheid means, among other things, to define and treat all our people as equal citizens of our country, without regard to race, color or ethnicity. To guarantee this, the ANC accepts that a new constitution for South Africa could include an entrenched Bill of Rights to safeguard the rights of the individual. We are, however, opposed to any attempt to perpetuate the apartheid system by advancing the concept of so-called group and minority rights.

Our region is fully conversant with the treacherous and deceitful nature of the apartheid regime. There are more than enough examples of agreements which this regime has shamelessly dishonored. Taking this experience into account, we insist that before any negotiations take place, the apartheid regime would have to demonstrate its seriousness by implementing various measures to create a climate conducive to such negotiations.

These would include the unconditional release of all political prisoners, detainees, all captured freedom fighters and prisoners of war as well as the cessation of all political trials. The state of emergency would have to be lifted, the army and the police withdrawn from the townships and confined to their barracks. Similarly, all repressive legislation and all laws empowering the regime to limit freedom of assembly, speech, the press and so on, would have to be repealed. . . .

There is, as yet, no prospect for genuine negotiations because the Botha regime continues to believe that it can maintain the apartheid system through force and terror. We therefore have no choice but to intensify the mass political and armed struggle for the overthrow of the illegal apartheid regime and the transfer of power to the people.

We also call on all our people to reject and spurn Botha's so-called National Council and make certain that this apartheid council never sees the light of day.

We reiterate our appeal to the international community to join us in this noble struggle by imposing comprehensive and mandatory sanctions against racist South Africa to end the apartheid system and reduce the amount of blood that will otherwise have to be shed to achieve this goal.

22

UNITED DEMOCRATIC FRONT

Ya, the Community Is the Main Source of Power
March 1986

In its scope and variety, the United Democratic Front is comparable only to Solidarity in Poland in the martial-law period. Founded in 1983, the UDF had two basic aims. On the one hand, the organization sought to unite the population—which, even under apartheid, was inclined toward passive acceptance of a harshly restrictive system—against the regime. The organization's slogan "UDF Unites, Apartheid Divides" expressed this idea. On the other hand, the UDF aimed to harass the regime through a wide variety of generally peaceful tactics, which though coordinated in the underground required citizens to take an open stand. Both aims were sometimes belied in practice. From 1985 onward, some UDF activists engaged in horrific retributive violence in which political opponents or suspected police informers were killed. The propensity toward violent means is alluded to in this interview with an activist in the Eastern Cape. The interview directly addresses only one aspect of the UDF's work: the self-governing of townships.

From "Ya, the Community Is the Main Source of Power," *Isizwe* 1, no. 2 (March 1986): 35–40. Obtained from http://www.aluka.org.

Question: Comrade,[1] please can you tell us how are area committees elected?

Answer: We start at the street level. People gather themselves from the street and hold a meeting where they will decide. They elect their committee of ten people. Above that street level, the two townships (Kwanobuhle and Langa) are zoned into five areas each. Each area committee has ten members elected from street committees. There is also a committee co-ordinating all ten areas. But the apartheid system is trying very hard to demolish the area committees.

Question: They know all about it?

Answer: Yes . . . they wanted to know and harass and detain people involved in area committees. They ask all about this thing, and they threatened people saying "No this is indeed a communist orientation."

Question: What is the main role of the area committee?

Answer: It involves a political and social role in controlling and reducing crime. It's also where they discuss day-to-day problems of people. It's where even their organizations are able to get a mandate from the people—through the area committees. . . .

Question: You say area committees control crime. Can you give an example?

Answer: They are not trying to imitate the white courts, or trying to beat people. . . . No such thing. They are there to create peace among people. If there is something going to happen they call the people involved together and try to end it. . . . For instance a theft. If one steals a thing, if you can solve that, to have the thing returned back to the owner, you try. You talk to the one who steals. Also, even disputes of divorce. We try to involve relatives of both parties so that they can come together to find a solution. In cases of assault, we call those people involved, and try to talk them into paying medical fees for the assault. We tend to have success, and get a chance now to educate people about our cause.

Question: What do you say to such people?

Answer: We say that fighting each other, like doing harm to each other, the oppressed people, it doesn't help. The major thing people must concentrate on [is] fighting the apartheid system. So people

---

[1]Many in the resistance to apartheid adopted this form of greeting from the Communists, even if they were not members of the party.

must give their attention straight to the oppressive system. Some people are individualistic. So we're trying hard with these people to show them the right way. And now, with these area committee structures the crime rate is down—very, very down. . . . After a month of the area committees being formed, we got a report that there were two week-ends without any case of people being stabbed or assaulted. It is true that the rate of alcohol is still very high. But we try even to organize the shebeeners.[2] We have a specific time, at 9 o'clock they must be closed. They abide by that.

Question: Does the area committee operate like a court sometimes, or like a police force? Can you compare it with any of those?

Answer: You see, there are those called *amabutho*. They call themselves the police or army of the people. For instance, *amabutho* are the ones to avail themselves to patrol, when to check that the shebeeners are closed at 9 o'clock. That thing helped, because the owners of shebeens don't need to be told now. They know it is their responsibility to prevent crime from their place. . . . The only thing they do is separate the people. The kind of thing we emphasize to them is that we don't want people to be beaten up. But it has happened sometimes. For instance, I found one youth was being beaten up by the *amabutho* because he tried to enter the house of his girlfriend. The girl's mother reported him to the *amabutho*, who gave him lashes. I personally went to the *amabutho* and told them, "Look we must not do that. And now you do the same to the people, as the police do. The people will strike you off from the membership of the organizations of the people. If people decide on that, you will be aware that you are not doing this violence as part and parcel of the organization. You are doing violence without a mandate."

We are fighting for the liberation of our people. We must not ill-treat them. If we do something which is misconduct over them, they will run away from us. I told the *amabutho* this very important thing. We must get people to support us 100 percent. We don't need 99 percent. We want 100 percent. We must show the world the apartheid government stands alone.

Question: How is the *amabutho* composed? Is it youth?

Answer: Yes, it is the youth. The *amabutho* are people who volunteer, as soldiers of the people, and you find they have a pride for that.

---

[2]*shebeen*: an unlicensed bar, usually in the black townships.

Question: Do you politicize the *amabutho*?

Answer: Yes, we have to tell them about the past of the struggle, the history. We teach them you can't achieve anything without discipline.

Generally, ya, I can say the community is the main source of power, because the state has really lost the control over the people. He has no power over the people in terms of controlling them. This is why the people have formed these area committees, so that they can try to control themselves. What has been preached in the past about the Freedom Charter, even now we are trying to do that practically.

Question: Do the people know the Freedom Charter quite well in the townships of Uitenhage[3]?

Answer: They know the Freedom Charter, but especially the first clause, "The People Shall Govern."

---

[3] *Uitenhage*: an industrial city in what is now the Eastern Cape Province.

23

ALISON OZINSKY

Purple Reign

November 1989

In early 1988, government authorities banned the UDF, detained most of its leaders, and shut down its publications. The government sought also to recapture passive support, scheduling city elections in which each racial group could vote, albeit separately. Yet the UDF's network of hundreds of local organizations continued to exist. These organizations spearheaded a successful boycott of the elections, thus revealing that, as in Solidarity's Poland, habits of noncompliance had become ingrained. Out of this boycott was born the Mass Democratic Movement (MDM), which initiated an action called the Defiance Campaign in the fall of 1989. On September 2, four days before the planned election, MDM organized a protest march in Cape Town. Like the Orange Alternative in Poland, these marchers found a way to use the regime's chosen color (in this case, purple dye) against it. The regime quickly conceded defeat: State president F. W. de Klerk gave permission for a march in Cape Town on the 13th. Some 35,000, including Archbishop Desmond Tutu, marched under the slogan "Loop Kaapstad Oop" (Walk Cape Town Open) — in other words, force freedom by participation. One observer commented, "How will they ever be able to justify the police ever again breaking up a peaceful protest?"[1]

Friday's *Weekly Mail* Classifieds carried the advert: "You know who you are. You are beautiful and delicious. Meet me in Greenmarket Square at 11 a.m. on Saturday." Saturday morning you can hardly move amongst the fleamarket stalls for the men and women in blue.

[1] Dene Smuts and Shauna Westcott, eds., *The Purple Shall Govern: A South African A to Z of Nonviolent Action* (Cape Town: Oxford University Press, 1991), 82; Jeremy Seekings, *The UDF: A History of the United Democratic Front in South Africa, 1983–1991* (Athens: Ohio University Press, 2000), 254.

From Alison Ozinsky, "Purple Reign," *Upfront*, November 1989. Reprinted in *The Purple Shall Govern: A South African A to Z of Nonviolent Action*, ed. Dene Smuts and Shauna Westcott (Cape Town: Oxford University Press, 1991), 13–15.

Every corner holds a crowd of policemen struggling for pavement space. Suspicious security branch types sporting anoraks slouch against the windows of the coffee shops and mutter into walkie-talkies.

MDM marshalls face the unenviable task of identifying potential marchers milling on Greenmarket Square and ushering them into a nearby church hall from where the march will begin.

Inside I can hardly believe that a church hall can be so full and small and tense. People are sitting three to a chair and overflowing on to the floor. . . .

The theme of the march is "The people shall govern." We intend to march to parliament in arm-linked rows of eight behind our chosen dignitaries and representatives. If the police order us to disperse, we will sit down to kneel in the road. Kneel in the road? Nothing on earth will persuade me to kneel on the road in front of a serious mean-looking police force. My stomach contracts with fear and doubt. I look around and see my own expression on other faces and I am temporarily reassured.

Walking out of the church into Burg Street is like the moment before jumping from a high place. All of us know exactly what is outside. I hope that all the others are braver than me. There's still time to pull out. The rows are forming and my elbow forms a link. Figuratively, we close our eyes and take deep breaths and launch ourselves forward. The crowd of Saturday morning spectators is huge, the pavements are spilling over with curious shoppers. At the end of the road, the police are six deep and waiting. I see no quirts or batons. I wonder what they have in store for us. Will we just be led right through the phalanx of policemen? Predictably, our march grinds to a halt as we are given ten minutes to disperse.

The whole march sits down in the road and the tension mounts as our leaders negotiate with the police to continue to parliament. The crowd of supporters is clapping slowly and cheering.

Now we see what the ten minutes was all about. The yellow pride of Caledon Square[2] careens down the road flashing its lights. A soft noise of hydraulics and the nozzle of the infamous water cannon is aimed at the crowd. The marchers brace themselves. Somewhere a crucial button is pushed and a sharp jet of water bursts forth, changing in mid-stream to lurid purple.

Some are hit head on, full in the face. Some are knocked off their knees. Scramble and panic and somebody is shouting "Sit down, sit

---

[2]*yellow pride of Caledon Square*: the South African police, whose Cape Town headquarters are on Caledon Square and who used yellow vehicles in the apartheid period.

down." Some are pinned against the wall and are painted like paper dolls as the jet sweeps past. A small remaining huddle in the road are covering their heads under the purple spray.

The supply of purple dye seems endless and the machine sprays on and on. The gutters run with oily foam. The crowd is stunned into strange silence. All we can do is watch this weird purple blast sweep backwards and forwards. The church facade is transformed in strange slow motion from grey to psychedelic in a flourish of the jet. It seems as if it will never end.

Then it stops.

A lone protester has climbed on top of the truck and is diverting the nozzle away from the people. He is struggling with it, fighting with it, and the purple jet streaks wildly across the buildings. The crowd stares for a moment in disbelief—then goes wild, cheering, shouting and leaping in the air with delight for this brave young man.

It is an indescribable moment. Even the policemen can only stand and stare, seeming to have momentarily lost their grip on the situation.

Not for long. They retaliate as teargas billows into the square. Marchers and policemen alike are stumbling and choking and fighting for breath. Spectators have become participants, willingly or not.

Media reports can't possibly describe the shock and pain of being teargassed—what feels like an acute asthma attack. Some collapse in the road. Eyes streaming, nose and mouth and lungs burning, we run up streets, into buildings, it's like a war.

It is a war, and it feels like the city is on our side.

A friend of mine seeks refuge in a hairdressing salon and is washed clean of his purple stains. Another is rescued by taxi and whisked off down the back streets. A department store is used as a hideout and a comrade emerges with a clean pair of trousers.

We hear that all purple people are being rounded up and arrested. Jackets and jerseys are turned inside out and incriminating stains are quickly concealed. . . .

If it was a war, then peaceful protest was the victor. Not a stone was thrown. The feeling of unity and friendship in the city was real and very tangible.

By Monday morning an efficient graffiti artist had said it for all of us: "The purple shall govern." I can believe it.

24

NELSON MANDELA

We Are Committed to Building a Single Nation in Our Country

February 25, 1990

When Nelson Mandela was released from prison on February 11, 1990, he immediately embarked on a journey across South Africa. In the course of his travels, he gave four speeches, one in each of the country's main provinces. In this way, he hoped to redefine South African unity— framed by the regime as a unity of whites—and to take charge of the political agenda. He became South Africa's de facto leader, consulting with the people and calling on them to take part in the common struggle. These speeches were really the beginning of Mandela's presidential campaign, leading to his victory in the election of April 27, 1994.

In his speech in the city of Durban in Natal Province, Mandela addressed the interethnic violence there, which was pitting ANC supporters against the Inkatha Freedom Party of Mangosuthu Buthelezi, chief of the KwaZulu bantustan. South African unity had always been one of Mandela's chief concerns, as could be seen in his famous words at his 1964 trial: "I have fought against white domination and I have fought against black domination. I have cherished the ideal of a democratic and free society in which all persons live together in harmony and with equal opportunities. It is an ideal which I hope to live for and to achieve. But if needs be, it is an ideal for which I am prepared to die." Like his counterparts in other revolutions, Mandela was looking beyond victory to the problems of governing a long-divided society.

From Nelson Mandela, "We Are Committed to Building a Single Nation in Our Country: Speech at Rally in Durban," in Nelson Mandela, *"Intensify the Struggle to Abolish Apartheid": Speeches, 1990* (New York: Pathfinder, 1990), 31, 34–39.

Friends, comrades, and the people of Natal, I greet you all. I do so in the name of *peace*, the peace that is so desperately and urgently needed in this region.

In Natal, apartheid is a deadly cancer in our midst, setting house against house and eating away at the precious ties that bind us together. This strife amongst ourselves wastes our energy and destroys our unity. My message to those of you involved in this battle of brother against brother is this: take your guns, your knives, and your *pangas* [machetes]. And throw them into the sea. Close down the death factories. *End this war now!*

We also come together today to renew the ties that make us one people, and to reaffirm a single united strand against the oppression of apartheid. . . .

The ANC offers a home to all who ascribe to the principles of a free, democratic, nonracial, and united South Africa. We are committed to building a single nation in our country. Our new nation will include blacks and whites. Zulus and Afrikaners, and speakers of every other language. . . .

Our call is "one nation, one country." *We must be one people across the whole of South Africa!*[1]

Yet even now as we stand together on the threshold of a new South Africa, Natal is in flames. Brother is fighting brother in wars of vengeance and retaliation. Every family has lost dear ones in this strife. In the last few years of my imprisonment, my greatest burden, my deepest suffering, was caused by the reports which reached me of the terrible things which were happening to you people here in Natal. . . .

It is my duty to remind you now, in the middle of your great sufferings, of the responsibility which we bear today. If we do not bring a halt to this conflict, we will be in grave danger of corrupting the proud legacy of our struggle. We endanger the peace process in the whole of the country.

Apartheid is not yet dead. Equality and democracy continue to elude us. We do not have access to political power. We need to intensify our struggle to achieve our goals. But we cannot do this as long as the conflict amongst ourselves continues. . . .

Our search for peace is a search for strength.

As a result of our historic struggles, we in the Mass Democratic Movement and in the ANC are the premier political force in the country.

---

[1] Italicized text, here and later in the document, was spoken in Zulu.

This preeminence confers on us responsibilities over and above the concerns of power politics. We have a duty to look beyond our own ranks and our immediate concerns. We must strive more earnestly to unite all the people of our country, and to nurture that unity into a common nationhood. Wherever divisions occur, such as in the strife here in Natal, it is a reflection against us and our greater societal goals. . . . We need to be rigorous in identifying our own contribution to the escalation of violence wherever it may occur. We have a greater purpose than the defeat of rival oppressed groups. It is the creation of a healthy and vibrant society.

We condemn, in the strongest possible terms, the use of violence as a way of settling differences amongst our people. *Great anger and violence can never build a nation. The apartheid regime uses this strife as a pretext for further oppression.* . . .

The Freedom Charter asserts that there should be houses, security, and comfort for all. We demand that the government provide these basic necessities of life. *The shortage of housing, water, and work opportunities, the forced removal of people, and the destruction of their houses: these are our problems. They must not make us enemies.* . . .

It is thus vital that we end the conflict in Natal, and end it now. Everyone must commit themselves to peace. Women of Natal, in the past and at crucial moments, you have shown greater wisdom than your menfolk. . . .

I charge you with a special responsibility here today. It is you, in your wisdom now, who must begin the work of bringing peace to Natal. Tell your sons, your brothers, and your husbands, that you want peace and security. It is you who must show them the real enemy. *All women know of mass poverty and homelessness, of children dying from diseases caused by hunger, poverty, and repression. We must therefore end the strife and the fighting and the misunderstanding in the community so that we defeat our common enemy, the apartheid regime.* Open the cooking pots and ask them why there is so little food inside. When the rains come into your homes, place the hands of your men in the pools on the floor, and ask them: "Why?" When your child ails, and you have no money to take it to a doctor, ask them: "Why?" There is only one answer, and that answer is our common deprivation. Go out and meet the women of the other side. Their story is the same. Then take your men with you.

I want to hear from you. From each and every community, I want a report. I want to hear the story of how you made the peace. We place our trust in you.

...We are many thousands gathered here in this stadium today. Let us now pledge ourselves to peace and to unity. Join hands all of you and raise them up for all to see.

A great deal of energy has been wasted by our people in violent actions across the towns and villages of this province. If we could channel this energy towards the real enemy of the people—apartheid—we could be free within days.

We have already waited for our freedom for far too long. We can wait no longer. Join forces, Indians, Coloureds, Africans, and freedom-loving whites, to give apartheid its final blow. In the process, let us develop active democracy. Democratic structures which serve the people must be established in every school, township, village, factory, and farm.

Since my release, I have become more convinced than ever that the real makers of history are the ordinary men and women of our country. Their participation in every decision about the future is the only guarantee of true democracy and freedom. Undue reliance should not be placed on the goodwill of the government. It is still a white minority regime concerned to protect white minority rights as far as it can. Nor should our reliance be placed on the abilities of the statesmen amongst us and our political leaders to negotiate an acceptable settlement. It is only the united action of you, the people, that will ensure that freedom is finally achieved. I call, therefore, for an all-round intensification of our struggle. *Together we shall conquer!*

Mayibuye i-Afrika! Amandla![2]

---

[2]*Mayibuye i-Afrika! Amandla!*: Xhosa chants traditional at ANC rallies: "Let it return! Africa! Power!"

6

Ukraine, 1987–1991

The breakup of the Soviet Union was both a cause and an effect of the democratic revolutions of the late 1980s. As we have seen, Mikhail Gorbachev hoped to save the Soviet Union by reforming it; instead, he presided over its demise. A union of fifteen republics that had seemed unshakable at the beginning of 1989 had disappeared from the map by the end of 1991. In its place were fifteen new countries, none of which had been independent for at least fifty years.

Things could have turned out quite differently. After all, nonviolent transformation requires commitment on both sides; it is not enough for an opposition to decide against armed conflict if leaders do not also take that step. To some extent, leaders can be swayed by the behavior of opposition or by external pressures; these factors can be seen in a number of the cases in this book. A peaceful conclusion was perhaps least likely in the Soviet case given the threat that the opposition posed not just to the regime but to the country itself and to relations among ethnic groups.

This central event in global political transformation is not easy to represent as a revolution. Most of the fifteen newly independent states, including Russia and the states of Central Asia and the Caucasus, cannot really be said to have undergone a transition to democracy, though in each the level of freedom is now greater than it was thirty years ago. The most successful revolutions—the Baltic states of Estonia, Latvia, and Lithuania—lack the global significance of other case studies. Ukraine, which was the second most populous of the Soviet republics, offers the most insight into how politics changed in the Soviet Union. Though it may not have seemed so at the time, twenty years later it is becoming clear that Ukraine has undergone the most dramatic transformation of the group.

Ukraine had become Soviet in stages. At the time of the Russian Revolution (1917), a West Ukrainian National Republic flashed briefly on the horizon before the Red Army on one side, and Poland on the other, divided up Ukraine. Collectivization of agriculture under Joseph Stalin in the 1930s, and the resultant famine, ravaged Ukrainian society, as did purges of national and local leaders. After World War II, the Soviet Union took from Poland the territory of Eastern Galicia (including the city of L'viv, long the heart of Ukrainian nationalism). The purges continued, accompanied by Russification that reduced Ukrainian to the status of a local language whose literature survived largely in exile and in the labor camps of Siberia.

Ukrainians were among the first to respond to the Helsinki Accords of 1975 (see Introduction), seeing the international recognition of human rights as a tool to reassert national rights. But members of the Ukrainian Helsinki Group (Document 26), among them Vyacheslav Chornovil, quickly found themselves imprisoned. Two factors reawakened opposition in Ukraine in the early years of Gorbachev's administration. The first of these was a revived tradition of dissent, as Chornovil and others returned home to L'viv or to the capital, Kyiv, and decided to test the limits of Gorbachev's *glasnost* (see Document 7). The second was the explosion at the nuclear power plant at Chernobyl (Ukrainian: Chornobyl') in northern Ukraine in April 1986. While open protests were rare, the disaster lent urgency to political activism.

Gorbachev took steps to rein in nationalist dissent, especially in the Baltic republics where national opposition was better organized; like any good Communist, he regarded nationalism as a reactionary, elitist force. Yet his increasingly evident willingness to rethink the Soviet economic and political system opened the door for ever-stronger moves for autonomy, especially in republics where opposition was already well organized. In March 1989, elections to the Congress of People's Deputies allowed for multiple candidates for the first time in Soviet history. Though there could be no opposition parties, many Ukrainian advocates of national autonomy (no one was yet talking about independence) ran for seats as representatives of a new umbrella group, the National Movement for Support of Perestroika (usually called simply *Rukh*, "Movement"), and some were elected. As members of parliament, they now had access to television and sharpened their demands for autonomy. A new dynamic emerged in the politics of the Soviet republics: Communist party leaders now actually attempted to gain popularity, painting themselves as advocates of national autonomy. Lithuania and Latvia even declared independence in March 1990, though the world largely ignored them. Ukraine followed in July with a declaration of sovereignty that, while not going as far as the Baltics had, asserted that Ukrainian law superseded Soviet law and that Ukraine had the right to self-determination.

Gorbachev now began an attempt to recast the Soviet Union through a new treaty that would give the republics far-reaching autonomy. The day before it was to be signed, August 19, 1991, a group of Communist party leaders opposed to this liberalization staged a coup to overthrow Gorbachev. The coup failed, but it spelled the end of the Soviet Union. The republics now rushed for the exits, led by Ukraine, which declared independence just a few days later. Gorbachev formally dissolved the Soviet Union in December.

Between 1987 and 1990, Ukrainian society relearned self-organization after decades of Sovietization. Yet the abruptness of the Soviet Union's collapse, as well as the strategic importance that Ukraine continued to have for Moscow, stunted Ukraine's democratic transformation. Its leaders, especially President Leonid Kuchma (1994–2005), proved increasingly corrupt, authoritarian, and beholden to Moscow. Another revolution, the Orange Revolution of November and December 2004, would be needed to push Ukraine toward democracy. Yet that revolution, whose outcome remains uncertain, would not have been possible without the prior experience of democratic change.

Reading these documents, consider what might explain Ukraine's more modest success in comparison with other cases. What role might the demands and visions of the opposition play? For example, how do Vyacheslav Chornovil's concerns and ideas compare with those of Aung San Suu Kyi or Václav Havel? The documents in this chapter express fears about national, cultural, and even biological survival. How does the conception of what a nation is and who its members are differ from ideas articulated in other cases?

25

VYACHESLAV CHORNOVIL

Open Letter to Mikhail Gorbachev

1987

Vyacheslav Chornovil (1937–1999), a journalist by profession, was Ukraine's best-known dissident. He was a founding member and editor of the opposition journal Ukrainian Herald *and a founding member of the Ukrainian Helsinki Group, formed in 1976 to call attention to human rights abuses. Though he was never a member of the Communist party, his open letter shows a genuine belief that the party's leader, Mikhail Gorbachev, deserved support; he is careful to couch his letter in the language of Soviet politics. With this letter, Chornovil also expresses his belief that open activity was the best form of opposition.*

The whole world is following with great interest your attempts to put into practice some democratic ideas that are new for Soviet society. And though you call the current changes in the country revolutionary, unfortunately one has to concur that at the moment it is only "a revolution in words." It is obvious that you do not have enough active and honest partners and helpers to break the resilient back of the Soviet party bureaucracy. Their numbers would increase if you were to stop stifling and putting on the back burner such important problems in *perestroika* as the right to free criticism, legal opposition and the national question.

Allow me to share some thoughts with you as a competent person who, over the past twenty years, has been among "dissidents" and "nationalists" and who has experienced nearly the whole arsenal of restraints on independent thinking (except perhaps for "psychiatric" incarceration): prohibition to practice a profession; administrative surveillance; harassment of family and friends; four trials (among them one on a flimsily constructed criminal charge), fifteen years of prison, camps and exile, etc. . . .

From "Open Letter to M. Gorbachev from Vyacheslav Chornovil," in *Dissent in Ukraine under Gorbachev*, ed. Taras Kuzio (London: Ukrainian Press Agency, 1989), 3–8, 10, 12.

Views on the problems of the national economy in the Soviet Union, criticism of language policies in the republics, for which we were carted off to prison camps until not long ago, are now being repeated from public platforms and in the press by leading Soviet writers. . . .

It is a logical conclusion that the social, political, spiritual and economic stagnation of the last twenty years was precisely the result of the harsh suppression of all independent thinking, the spirit of criticism and doubt. And it is equally logical to assume that the official *glasnost*, regimented and under control of the party organs, will be inadequate for the spiritual relief of the society and insufficient to move forward. Inevitably, what could be called dissent, legal opposition or simply independent criticism in one form or another will have to be allowed. If you need some confirmation from Lenin in these cases then you could refer to his tolerance towards opposition and oppositionists in the party, how he advised searching for the grain of truth even in the criticisms of the emigre press, how he taught his colleagues and followers: "it is not necessary to assume 'intrigue' or 'opposition' in those who think and act differently, but to value independent people."[1]

. . . Even now, some political prisoners, victims of the period of stagnation where there was no *glasnost*, continue to study your speeches on democratic renewal of Soviet society through fortified prison bars; others were given their freedom as a favor (although the confessions and pleas for mercy should have come from their tormentors). A third category, having served the full term of imprisonment, continue to face discrimination of a different nature. An example is close at hand: tomorrow morning, I, a former journalist in republic and regional newspapers and television, publicist and literary critic, will change shifts at my work as a stoker with a former instructor of the regional party committee. After him will come a doctoral candidate in philology, university lecturer, author of verses for which he was arrested and sentenced to a term not much less than mine—twelve years. . . . The situation is the same for many others who have been freed.[2] . . .

---

[1] *Vladimir Lenin* (1870–1924): leader of the Communist party of the Soviet Union (CPSU). Chornovil purposely places Lenin, usually considered no friend of dissent and democracy, in an unfamiliar light. The quote is from Lenin's letter to N. Osinsky, December 1921, in Lenin, *Collected Works*, v. 45 (Moscow, 1970), p. 406.

[2] As in Czechoslovakia, where Václav Havel (Document 1) was sent to work in a brewery, political opponents in the Soviet Union were often barred from their chosen professions and assigned menial labor, such as the tending of coal furnaces.

In this situation, let me remind you that any creative individual, be he a stoker or carpenter, will always need to find an outlet for his creative energy and intellectual potential. And if you do not wish to channel this creativity within this democratic restructuring of society, then we will find our own readers, observers and listeners.

I am informing you that several Ukrainian journalists and writers, who are presently experiencing a ban on their works and within their profession, including myself in this work, are legally reviving the publication of the socio-political and literary journal, *The Ukrainian Herald*, which appeared from 1970–1972 under difficult circumstances. This journal wholly conforms to the present stipulations of *"glasnost."*

There is also the idea of forming our own creative circles independent from the official ones, which enforce a ban upon us, and forming our own associations of persecuted Ukrainian writers, journalists, artists even though the circulation of our publications may well be limited; we would also organize exhibitions in private apartments, and if the opportunity arose, we would consider publishing our works or organizing exhibitions abroad, without any intention of going against the state. That is the legal right of any author.

We hope that you and the Politburo of the Central Committee of the CPSU will appreciate our efforts to allow our society to witness this true *"glasnost."*

If one sees a positive result on the question of independent thought (i.e. the release of some political prisoners, the immediate halting of repressions, the taciturn admittance—so far only from the center—of various democratic forms of opposition, such as demonstrations, legal *samvydav*,[3] etc.), then the national question has ended up in the deafest corner of this *perestroika* even though this is a most vital question for this multi-national country which has proclaimed itself as the Union of Sovereign Socialist Republics. . . .

In practice, *perestroika* in the national question is limited at the moment to the opportunity for activists in national cultures, primarily writers, to talk (on a superficial level without going into substance or circumstances, without mentioning the total or even partial dissolution of the state functions of supposedly sovereign nations) about the depressed situation of national languages and the cultural heritage of their people. . . .

---

[3] Ukrainian for *samizdat* (see Document 1), self-published works.

In order to return to Lenin's norm with respect to nationality policies the initiatives ought to come from the ranks of the Soviet party leadership. . . . It is necessary to hold a special plenum of the Central Committee of the Communist Party of Ukraine where, with the same courage and openness you showed at the June plenum in your speech about the economy,[4] one could openly discuss the true situation of the non-Russian nationalities in the USSR, the fictitious character of their sovereignty and the total non-conformity to Lenin's mandates, particularly as stated in his well-known work, "The question of nationality or autonomy."[5] . . .

I would dearly want to believe that now under the auspices of this new democracy publicly initiated by you, Moscow will finally extend, to its "younger" brothers in this Union of "equal rights," its hand without the traditional iron fist.

. . . First and foremost, it is essential to extend the rights of the republics of the Soviet Union with respect to political, economical and cultural life. . . . Secondly, it is vital to return to its fullest extent the usage of national languages within the state and community framework. To this end, within the republics' constitutions, national languages must again be proclaimed as state languages and this must be put into practice. . . .

They will try to alarm you with claims of "bourgeois nationalism" and even the break-up of the Soviet Union although the policy is aimed at strengthening it as an actual, and not fictitious, union. Only in this way will it be possible to overcome the fierce opposition of the Russian and Russified bureaucracies. But, believe me, you will find understanding among the greater part of the Russian nation not yet tainted by chauvinism, however in the other republics, you will receive the most fervent support and see an outburst of creative energy within all aspects of *perestroika*. As representatives of the non-Russian sector of the Soviet Union population, we will ultimately only accept this *perestroika* as our own once it is carried out not only in the interest of all the classes and strata of society (except the bureaucrats) but in the interest of all the nations and nationalities of the Soviet Union.

[4]At a plenum of the Central Committee of the Communist party of the Soviet Union in June 1987, Gorbachev devoted his remarks to the need to restructure the economy.

[5]Lenin expressed concerns about Russian domination over other national groups in an article published in December 1922.

26

UKRAINIAN HELSINKI UNION

Atomic Evil Out of Ukraine!

November 1988

The Chernobyl disaster of April 1986 had three effects on political change in Ukraine. First, it made apathy or conformity impossible for many Ukrainians (and others in the region, too): One might resign oneself to the lack of the Ukrainian language in one's children's school but draw the line at accepting a threat to people's very lives. This petition, issued by the Ukrainian Helsinki Union (known before 1988 as the Ukrainian Helsinki Group), spoke to the fears of ordinary citizens of Ukraine. Second, opposition activists interpreted the event as a crime not only against the environment and the people but against the nation, placing its very existence in peril; it thus helped to fuse democratic and nationalist opposition. Finally, Chernobyl jolted Gorbachev out of complacent expectation that the Soviet Union would smoothly reform itself. The approach he took in his speech to the Communist party plenum, excerpted in Document 7, was partially a result of this realization. Anti-Communist activists in many republics, like those in Poland, as we saw earlier, sought to capitalize on all of these trends.

An Appeal from the Executive Committee of the Ukrainian Helsinki Union

Citizens of Ukraine!

The threat of destruction hangs over our country, the specter of degeneration over our people. As a result of the criminal centralist policies of the Stalinist-Brezhnevite leadership, which ignores the interests of the sovereign (on paper only) republics; as a result of the irresponsibility of the local authorities, who leased out Ukraine to the mafias in the ministries and departments, Ukraine is oversaturated with energy,

---

From Ukrainian Helsinki Union, "'Atomic Evil—Out of Ukraine!' The Ukrainian Helsinki Union Demands a Nuclear Free Ukraine!" in *Dissent in Ukraine under Gorbachev*, ed. Taras Kuzio (London: Ukrainian Press Agency, 1989), 38–39.

mining, metallurgical, and chemical industries, those that produce the greatest amounts of harmful wastes. Nearly 50% of the atomic energy output of the Soviet Union is concentrated in Ukraine.

The Chernobyl tragedy, which shook the entire world, taught the ruling bureaucratic leadership nothing. New atomic reactors are being built or planned for the Rivne, the Novo-Ukrayinka, the Khmelnytsk and the Zaporizhzhia atomic power stations. Despite protests by the community, the construction of the Crimean atomic power station is near completion, while in Chyhyryn, the very historical center of Ukraine, quietly like thieves they continue building an atomic power plant. And this is at a time when Ukraine even now exports electricity to other countries, when, with efficient management, a reduction in the energy requirements to world standards, the entire electrical energy output of Ukrainian atomic power plants would become superfluous. And this when atomic energy is banned in many countries or is being cut back, when such a superindustrial country as the U.S.A. has decided to renounce the further building of atomic power plants and shut down existing ones.

The time has come to put an end to predatory management practices in our land. At first we were forced to take pride in being the bread basket of Russia, then the all-Union forge and the all-Union boiler room. Today Ukraine is becoming the all-Union reactor, and, in perspective, the all-Union, and even the all-human cemetery. Today we are called upon to remind the rulers that this land has a master—**the people**, for whom it is not only the means of carrying out production plans, but also the historical cradle of the past, the native home in which present and future generations could live a life of happiness.

Glasnost brought the long overdue truth about the cruel thirties to the pages of our newspapers. But if we rejoice about the truth of the past alone then the years ahead will be even more horrific. Yes, the artificial famine of the thirties took eight million lives; the blood runs cold in the veins at the thought. But what about today's truth? Where is it? Why do they want to lull it to sleep, the truth about the seven and one half million who walk among us today and who, in the opinion of competent scientists, will be prematurely laid to rest in the earth? And this is only from one reactor in Chernobyl! But fifty have been planned for us!

Ukrainian scientists, writers and public figures appealed to the authorities and later to the 19th Conference of the ruling party, demanding that the further development of atomic energy in Ukraine be halted. The issue of a referendum was raised. However, as evidenced by the reaction to this appeal, or, more accurately, by the absence of any reaction whatsoever, no one has taken these demands seriously; no one even thinks about asking the people. Meanwhile the Ministry of Atomic Energy pushes forward by putting new reactors and new nuclear power plants into operation.

People! Let's stop the madmen! Let's stop them before it's too late!

May this collection of signatures become a national referendum by which the Ukrainian people and all other nationalities that live on the territory of Ukraine declare for life. Our land witnessed many enemy invasions. Our ancestors preserved it for us. Today the historical responsibility for Ukraine's fate falls with all its weight upon us. So let's defend our native land against the merciless talons of centralism and from our own irresponsibility and indifference to our fate, the fate of our children and grandchildren, the fate of our suffering land.

Kiev-L'viv, November 1988. . . .

Supporting the appeal by the Executive Committee of the Ukrainian Helsinki Union, we the undersigned, demand that the governments of the USSR and the Ukrainian SSR:

- Immediately halt the construction of the Crimean atomic power stations;
- Halt the operations of the Chernobyl atomic power stations;
- Develop and publicize a promising plan for the gradual elimination of all existing atomic power stations in Ukraine and their replacement by alternative means of generating electricity, as well as for the closing down of those production facilities that have great electrical energy requirements, are damaging to the environment and are located in zones of industrial overload and in densely populated areas.

Atomic evil—out of Ukraine!

27

Founding Meeting of the Native Language Association

June 13, 1988

Beginning in 1987, in the western city of L'viv, people who had never been engaged in opposition and who tended to be younger than the generation of Vyacheslav Chornovil began to organize. Among them was Ihor Mel'nyk, an engineer at the Kineskop factory. In early 1988, he began to collect signatures for a petition asking for permission to found a society to promote the Ukrainian language. City authorities reluctantly gave Mel'nyk permission to hold an inaugural meeting on June 13, but then they locked the doors of the building where the gathering was to take place. The crowd of supporters, a thousand or so, simply moved to the nearby square to hold a rally by the statue of writer Ivan Franko. Many leading dissidents addressed the crowd, including Mykhaylo Horyn' of the Helsinki Union and Iryna Kalynets', a leader in the opposition centered around the Ukrainian Greek Catholic Church, a religious faith based largely in western Ukraine. In this meeting, we can see a process of radicalization taking place as a crowd that has gathered for relatively innocuous purposes becomes a vessel for political opposition, in part because of the authorities' reaction.

Engineer Ihor Mel'nyk, a member of the initiative group forming the association, read the collectively written draft statute of the Native Language Association. . . .

Then Mykhaylo Horyn' spoke: "Esteemed comrades! The creation of the L'viv Native Language Association is one of the rungs of the ladder by which we will raise our consciousness, which has fallen so low it is difficult to imagine. How many of our children have turned away from their language, how many of our brothers and sisters have forgotten their birthplace? But we are beginning to awaken. I support what has been read out here, but I believe that such a society should

From "Mityng bilia pam'iatnyka I. Frankovi 13.VI.88 r. (skorochennyi zapys)," in *Desiat' dniv, shcho skolykhnuly L'viv* . . . (New York: Zakordonnyi predstavnytstva Ukraïnskoï helsinskoï spilki, 1989), 12–14, 16–19. Translated by Padraic Kenney.

set serious goals. I propose adding a paragraph about expanding the sphere of native language use, since this has already been expressed even in the newspapers: The association will fight for the Ukrainian language's status as the official language of the Ukrainian Republic.... As we discuss the question of the status of the Ukrainian language, we must talk about ensuring that it is used. The Ukrainian language ought to be introduced into every institution, without exception: scientific institutes, management, administrative offices, etc. The job of the association is to bring the Ukrainian language into all spheres of society, into the workplace, into science and culture. And into politics, in fact. It would be very good, for example, if our Ukrainian Ministry of Foreign Affairs really dealt with foreign affairs and did not just sit around playing cards. We should insist that the administrative bureaucracy, which is in fact incredibly Russified, should prepare its entire staff to be examined in knowledge of Ukrainian."

A voice from the crowd: "If you want to eat, learn!"

Horyn': "I'm not saying anything new.... This is not a discriminatory proposal, but is of elementary importance for this nation, whom you administer and whose bread you eat. Last Saturday and Sunday, here in L'viv, there was a conference of representatives of independent organizations, at which was discussed the problem of national construction in the republics. The conference was convened at the initiative of the *Ukrainian Herald* and the Ukrainian Helsinki Group.... As I listened for two days to what they are doing in the Baltic republics and the Caucasus, I was ashamed for us. Even here, colleagues whom we have just elected [to the association] did not want to come out and show themselves in public—this certainly is not a good start to the association's work. I hope that though the shirt of fear now is stuck to our spine, it will start to loosen in the course of our work, and we will become normal people...."

A woman's voice: "Such people should be excluded—don't select them!"

Horyn': "We all understand clearly that language is only a part of the larger, complex Ukrainian problem. If the administrative and management bureaucracy has no need for professionals who know Ukrainian, we will become just a bunch of dilettantes. We must change the question from a purely cultural one into a political one and declare that industry, and all other branches [of the economy] should *Ukrainianize*! This is one of the proposals to emphasize what is written in our constitution: that we have a Union of states, not of provinces. We should demand that this state, which we call Ukraine, be an authentic

state within the conditions that exist. We need to work hard in this
direction—other republics are ahead of us."

Next, Iryna Kalynets' spoke: "Something doesn't get done just by
talking about it. There are a lot of us here—and let everyone think
about what concretely he can do in the association. Who can assemble
examination commissions, who can sign up to give cultural performances, who can travel about and give lectures? There should be a
statute, and now we must put together a program. Everyone must do
something. Go to the villages and inspire the people, go to the factories, talk with people. Do you understand? So everyone here needs to
say something of himself. Therefore we ask you: Write down in your
name, what you can do, what you propose." . . .

The resolution of the constituent assembly confirming the statute of
the Taras Shevchenko Native Language Association was accepted. . . .
Although the official part of the gathering was finished, the rally continued. People did not want to leave. . . .

Now Natalia Didchuk, a student at L'viv University, spoke: "I call all
of you my brothers, because you have stood up for our language, for
our culture, and for this, that in every home, in every family mothers
will be able to sing our beautiful lullabies to their children in their
native tongue. I would like for you to raise your voices so that our
Ukrainian Virgin Mary would no longer be called the Black Madonna
because of Chernobyl, or because of the pierced hearts of our boys in
Afghanistan.[1] Brothers! Let us consecrate these good beginnings to
the immortal memory of our fathers, who perished under Stalin, our
grandfathers, taken by war, and our great-grandfathers, also taken by
war. Let us not lose our roots, and remember that we are Ukrainians,
we are proud of this name." . . .

One after another, people got up on the improvised stage, around
the Franko monument, and read the verses on language by Sydir
Vorobkevych, Ivan Hnatiuk, Bogdan Stel'makh, and Volodymyr
Sosiura, and fragments of Taras Shevchenko's poem "To the Dead and
the Living."[2]

---

[1]The Soviet Union invaded Afghanistan in 1978. By the time Gorbachev began withdrawal in 1988, some 15,000 Soviet troops had been killed.
[2]Sydir Vorobkevych (1836–1903), Ivan Hnatiuk (1929–), Bogdan Stel'makh (1943–),
and Volodymyr Sosiura (1898–1965) are all Ukrainian poets and songwriters. Taras
Shevchenko (1814–1861) is widely considered Ukraine's greatest writer, the father of
modern Ukrainian literature.

28

IVAN DRACH

The Political Situation in Ukraine and Rukh's Task

October 1990

*As late as the summer of 1989, organized opposition in the Ukrainian
Soviet Socialist Republic was confined to intellectual elites and to the city
of L'viv. Rukh, the Ukrainian Popular Movement for Perestroika, began
to change this. As its name suggests, the movement positioned itself
within the political sphere but in support of Gorbachev. A republic-wide
strike by miners in the summer of 1989 moved protest onto a new plane,
as strikers, along with Adam Michnik of Poland, addressed Rukh's first
congress in September of that year. At the congress,* perestroika *disappeared from the movement's name, symbolizing its reorientation toward
purely Ukrainian matters. In 1990, elections at the republic and local
levels effectively broke the Communist party's monopoly on politics; the
Ukrainian parliament's near-unanimous passage of the Declaration of
Sovereignty in July 1990 showed that nationalism had become an
accepted language. At Rukh's second congress, its leader, Ivan Drach
(1936–), a poet from Kyiv, traced a vision of a united Ukrainian political opposition.*

Any objective historical, political, economic, social or cultural analysis
would inevitably lead us to the same conclusion: only the total sovereignty of the Ukrainian people, a completely independent Ukrainian
state, is appropriate given the present development of world civilization. Any other form of historical existence of the people, the nation,
would leave it with no choices, no mercy, throw Ukrainian society out
into the back yard of civilization, turn it into food, raw material,
resources to be used for the further development of other nations
which have their own states. This is the challenge that fate is sending

From "Drach's Opening Speech to Rukh Congress," in *JPRS Report: Soviet Union —
Political Affairs* 72 (December 28, 1990): 38–44.

us, this is the choice before which we stand. Either—or. We must understand this now, as we stand at the edge of the bottomless abyss of the union treaty.[1] If our souls and minds are not yet completely mutilated and plundered, we are obliged to be horrified by the current situation of the Ukraine, to finally learn something from her thousand-year history. Let us look into one hundred eyes, into 50 million eyes. . . .

Today, political and just plain human awakening is knocking at the door of every inhabitant of the Ukraine. The Donetsk miner, Lugansk chemist, Dnieper bank metallurgist, Kiev, Kharkov, Sumy machinist, Mykolayiv and Kherson ship builder, the conscientious and docile Poltava or Podillya grain and cattle farmer, the dweller of the coastline of the dying Black Sea or of the Dnieper, which has been turned into poisonous mud, not to mention those whose settlements have been transformed into an atomic leper colony by the cesium and strontium plague[2]—none of us here, in the Ukraine, can hide any longer, close our eyes, cover our ears and fail to hear the knocking on all of our doors by disablement, national death, degeneration, nonexistence. The present regime, which speaks in the words of the proletarian hymn, cares not about us. And it will never care about us. It is not ours. However much a meat processing plant may be reconstructed, it still remains a meat processing plant. Technological improvement can lighten the work of the staff or of the "collective management," allow the plant to enter the international market, increase profits, even "humanize" the barbaric slaughterhouse, but a people which cannot defend its own rights will always remain that plant's raw material. . . . We, Ukrainians, have paid God and humanity an unbelievable price for our existence. And we have the right to not bring any more bloody sacrifices onto the altar of our independence, we have paid for it one-hundred-fold. . . .

It is now completely obvious that after several years of official fireworks about *perestroika*, . . . in the summer of 1989 began the real *perestroika*, which was not expected by the authorities and was awaited by democratic forces: the appearance on the arena of political struggle of no less powerful a force than the working class. The miners' strikes, well-organized and determined, really shook the party-state authorities. . . . The democratic forces, particularly those in the

---

[1]At this time, representatives of the Soviet republics were negotiating an agreement on relations with the central government. It was this treaty whose signing was canceled due to the Moscow coup of August 1991.

[2]A reference to the Chernobyl explosion.

Ukraine, do not have the billions of the CPSU or the CPU (Communist Party of Ukraine); they do not distribute sausages and footwear, building materials and other resources. We could offer the miners only our moral and political support, our solidarity, and this we did. The authorities succeeded in misleading the miners, frightening them, like Little Red Riding Hood, with the wicked wolf—Rukh. Who won out of this? Let the miners themselves answer. . . .

What should the strategy and tactics of the democratic forces of the Ukraine be from now on? First of all, let us state directly and openly that they are totally, consciously, in principle opposed to the strategy of the repressive party rulers who still hold power in the republic today. . . . But our strategy does not foresee seizing power and it follows only the peaceful path of consolidating the sovereignty of the Ukrainian people. In contrast to the Ukrainian Communist Party, we do not impose our rule on the people; we do not call on the workers to follow our lead to a bright, but never attainable, future. . . . We see our strategy and tactics in going to the people, taking in their misery and pains, their longings, their current and historical interests and turning these things into political action. We will not imitate the bolsheviks, who seized power through conspiracy and bloody coup d'etat and then turned it against the people. Democratic forces can take power only at the will of the workers and their future rule must be under the people's control. . . .

These principles logically and inevitably set the line of the tactics of our political battle. They include making use of all treaties recognized by international law, the United Nations, the Helsinki Agreements and methods of non-violent but determined defense by the people of their inalienable rights. The arsenal of our peaceful means of struggle will include methods taken from the golden treasury of national liberation movements, in particular, various forms of civil disobedience which have been blessed by Mahatma Gandhi, Martin Luther King and other great sons of humanity. We will study and apply the victorious experience of the Polish "Solidarity" and the Czechoslovak citizens' forum,[3] the experience of patriots in Namibia[4] and supporters of Nelson Mandela. All of this should be added to the achievements of our own Ukrainian national

---

[3] *citizens' forum*: the Civic Forum created by Václav Havel and other Czech dissidents in November 1989 during the "Velvet Revolution."

[4] The South-West Africa People's Organization (SWAPO) carried out a guerrilla war against the occupying forces of South Africa for nearly a quarter-century before gaining Namibia's independence in March 1990.

liberation struggle and should help us to avoid past mistakes. We will also work with all elected bodies, from the parliament of the Ukraine to village councils, to make certain that they do not go back to being mere divisions of various party committees of the CPSU or of so-called "party forums." . . .

Against the repression and terror of the penal and military organizations of the CPSU—the KGB, the Ministry of Internal Affairs, the army—we will also apply extra-parliamentary methods of struggle, in union with the people, because the police state created by the party is directed not only against democratic activists. Its main target is the worker who wishes to live in dignity, like a human being. Strikes, meetings, demonstrations, pickets, petitions, refusal to pay taxes, to participate in the illegal expropriation by the party-state of agricultural and industrial production under the guise of state orders and so-called socialist obligation, suspension of payment for community services— all of these and other actions are an effective weapon for the liberation of workers, especially now, when the serf-creating guidelines of the so-called economic reform are aiming for an even greater impoverishment of the people. . . .

When spontaneous protest, the natural and invincible human drive to freedom and happiness, is united with organized political forces, the progress of history becomes less brutal, less merciless, although it still remains irreversible. . . .

The authorities want to deceive us with their lies—we will oppose them with knowledge of the truth; let us learn and let us teach others.

The authorities want to divide us—let us oppose them with the unity of our democratic forces.

The authorities are trying to turn our attention to secondary issues—let us oppose them by understanding the essential.

The authorities are implementing economic and ideological chaos—let us oppose them with the organization of our ranks.

The authorities threaten us with the Beijing scenario—let us oppose them with fearlessness and endurance on the pattern of Prague. . . .

Long live Rukh as a structure which constantly renews itself!

LONG LIVE THE UKRAINE!

7

China, 1986–1989

China, where a large urban social movement failed to bring any steps toward democracy, is clearly the exceptional case in this book. The contrast with the other cases is neatly captured by one date: June 4, 1989. On that Sunday morning, as Poles woke up to vote in a semi-free election that would eventually bring Solidarity to power and an end to Communist rule in all of Europe, Beijing was experiencing a brutal crackdown. Seven weeks of largely peaceful protest ended as soldiers moved into Tiananmen Square (the central square in Beijing and the largest public urban space in the world), killing hundreds of students and their supporters. Thus while Eastern Europe, along with so many other countries, chose a peaceful path toward democratic change, the leaders of China chose the opposite direction.

The easy answer to why things turned out differently could be that the Chinese dictatorship simply had more backbone, but this is an inadequate explanation. True, hard-liners in Romania and East Germany praised the Tiananmen crackdown and wished they could have done the same to their opponents. One can hear the same argument made about any revolution: If Nicholas II in Russia in 1917, or Louis XVI in France in 1789, had not been so weak and indecisive, then history would have taken a different course.

But by this point, we should recognize that the "weak man" theory of history is just the obverse of the "great man" theory and is no more satisfying. Even strong dictatorships are not capable of controlling their histories and are shaped by forces beyond (or only partially under) their control. It is important to study regime strategy and regime capabilities, but reliance on this explanation lets the historian off the hook too easily. Weak or indecisive regimes, after all, do not necessarily give way to democratic forces. So what happened in China? The documents in this chapter allow us to examine the strategies and goals of the student demonstrators.

The life experience of every Chinese citizen over age twenty-five in 1989 was shaped by what may have been the largest campaign of popular mobilization in world history: the Cultural Revolution of 1966–1976.

Encouraged by Communist party leader Mao Zedong, millions of students (many in their early teens) waged war on all that was "old" in China—old traditions, old ways of thinking, and even their elders. Students humiliated and tortured their teachers, destroyed cultural monuments, and closed down universities. Mao's death in 1976 brought the Cultural Revolution to an end and opened up a brief space for dissent, as we saw in Wei Jingsheng's essay (Document 2). But the experience, which was both exhilarating and frightening, was a paradoxical lesson both in the ability of ideas to move huge numbers of people and in the power of mobilized youth. Most of all for Chinese leaders and even some opponents, it was a lesson about the dangers of unfettered popular mobilization.

The new leader, Deng Xiaoping (1904–1997), initiated economic reforms and an opening to the West. These policies raised hopes (which Wei Jingsheng found dubious) that political reform would also be forthcoming. Questions raised by student protesters in late 1986, such as those expressed in Document 29, had the main effect of putting the regime's back up. A prominent reform proponent, Hu Yaobang, was forced to resign as party head. Protest thus remained relatively narrow in scope; the opposition was closely attuned to, even dependent on, the actions of regime leaders.

Hu's death on April 15, 1989, provided an opening for those who had continued to think about political change. The fact that it did tells us a lot about the limits of opposition in China. Hu Yaobang was no Benigno Aquino but merely an elderly Communist party official who had briefly appeared to be in favor of more reform than other top Communists. That a state funeral (and disputes over the conduct of the funeral) would provide an occasion for protest is also a reminder of the power of ritual in Chinese public life. Within days, tens of thousands of students were marching, usually toward Tiananmen Square. Hu's funeral in that square on April 22 crystallized the students' sense of a political opportunity, as three students dramatically approached the Great Hall of the People, where party leaders were assembled for the occasion, and knelt on the steps. Thus political theater played an important role in China as well.

The Chinese case raises one further, very important set of questions: What kind of change is most important, economic or political, and how are these two related? This issue concerned not only the regime itself but also its critics. Deng Xiaoping's modernization plans centered on the economy, which continued to be his focus after the suppression of the Tiananmen Movement. Ironically, then, it is the one failed revolutionary case in this book that raises the most important questions about the future of democratic revolution. We know that democratic revolutions are not inevitable, but are they even necessary? Today one could argue that China's emergence as a world economic force has made democratic reform less likely as people become content with a better standard of living. But one could also argue the opposite: that improved living standards eventually allow people to think about other things besides survival. There is evidence for both conclusions around the world today. Once again, however, it is worth remembering that economic conditions by themselves may only furnish the context for political change and that the ideas and actions of democratic social movements contribute more to the course of events.

In reading these documents, note the writers' relative lack of concern about economic issues. What are the students' main concerns, and how do these compare with dissidents' priorities in other cases? Also consider how students interact with or address their elders and superiors. How might these interactions yield clues to their expectations? Finally, sacrifice is an important theme in several of the documents. What does sacrifice mean to the students, and are there comparable ideas in other documents in this book?

29

FANG LIZHI

Democracy, Reform, and Modernization
November 18, 1986

Fang Lizhi, just a few months older than Václav Havel, was already well known around the world in the 1980s in his field of astrophysics — in fact, he was one of China's best-known scientists. In the early 1980s, influenced in part by his experiences visiting Western universities, he began to write about the importance of academic freedom. From there he increasingly

From Fang Lizhi, "Democracy, Reform, and Modernization," in Fang Lizhi, *Bringing Down the Great Wall: Writings on Science, Culture, and Democracy in China*, ed. James H. Williams (New York: Knopf, 1991), 166–72, 187–88.

focused on larger problems of democracy, on the one hand, and modernization, on the other. This speech to students at Shanghai University was one of a series that Fang gave in the fall of 1986, during a period of relative liberalization, that contributed to student protests that winter.

Much of what is wrong with socialism comes from subscribing to obsolete ideas, ideas without basis in either theory or fact. Yet we never change, because we've lived with these notions so long that we are no longer aware of them. I am like this myself. I used to think that many of our problems were just a consequence of the way things are, part of the natural order. But going abroad has changed my perspective drastically. Socialism has failed in China. Certainly there are many reasons for this failure, but beyond the shadow of a doubt, much of what we have done here is neither progressive nor socialist. On the contrary, it has been extremely backward and feudalistic.

. . . Our understanding of the concept of democracy is so inadequate that we can barely even discuss it. With our thinking so hobbled by old dogmas, it is no wonder we don't achieve democracy in practice. Not long ago it was constantly being said that calling for democracy was equivalent to requesting that things be "loosened up." . . .

I think that the key to understanding democracy lies first of all in recognizing the rights of each individual. Democracy is built from the bottom up. Every individual possesses certain rights, or to use what is a very sensitive expression indeed in China, everyone has "human rights." . . .

But perhaps we are starting to view the spiritual aspects of civilization a little differently. We are beginning to see "liberty, equality, and fraternity" as a positive spiritual heritage. Over the last thirty years it seemed that every one of these good words—liberty, equality, fraternity, democracy, human rights—was labeled bourgeois by our propaganda. What on earth did that leave for us? Did we really oppose all of these things? If anything we should outdo bourgeois society and surpass its performance in human rights, nor try to deny that human rights exist.

Democracy is based on recognizing the rights of every single individual. Naturally, not everyone wants the same thing, and therefore the desires of different individuals have to be mediated through a democratic process, to form a society, a nation, a collectivity. But it is only on the foundation of recognizing the humanity and the rights of each person that we can build democracy. However, when we talk about "extending democracy" here, it refers to your superiors "extending democracy" for you. This is a mistaken concept. This is not democracy. "Loosening up" is even worse. If you think about it, what it implies is that everyone is tied up very tightly right now, but if you stay put, we'll loosen the rope a little bit and let you run around. The rope used to be one foot long, now we'll make it five feet. This is a top-down approach. Democracy is first and foremost the rights of individuals, and it is individuals that must struggle for them. Expressions like "extending democracy" and "loosening up" would have you think that democracy can be bestowed upon us by those in charge. Nothing could be further from the truth. . . .

In democratic countries, democracy begins with the individual. *I* am the master, and the government is responsible to *me*. Citizens of democracies believe that the people maintain the government, paying taxes in return for services — running schools and hospitals, administering the city, providing for the public welfare. . . . A government depends on the taxpayers for support and therefore *has to be* responsible to its citizens. This is what people think in a democratic society. But here in China, we think the opposite way. If the government does something commendable, people say, "Oh, isn't the government great for providing us with public transportation." But this is really something it *ought* to be doing in exchange for our tax money. . . . You have to be clear about who is supporting whom economically, because setting this straight leads to the kind of thinking that democracy requires. Yet China is so feudalistic that we always expect superiors to give orders and inferiors to follow them. What our "spiritual civilization" lacks above all other things is the spirit of democracy. If you want reform — and there are more reforms needed in our political institutions than I have time to talk about — the most crucial thing of all is to have a democratic mentality and a democratic spirit.

An experience that I had in France exemplified the democratic spirit for me. Western Europe is now undergoing a lot of terrorist activity, and people are worried about it; there is strong public opinion in favor of a crackdown against terrorism. A Chinese graduate student in France told me that a recent wave of violence there, such as airport bombings, had led to proposed legislation requiring citizens to report anyone they suspect of involvement in terrorist activities to the police immediately. This seems natural to us in China: Sound the alarm, and put the whole country on alert. Therefore, I just assumed that the French would pass this law. But the student, to my great surprise, told me that after this bill was proposed, the National Assembly discussed it for a while and then voted it down. Why? The members obviously didn't veto it because they approve of terrorism. No, their reasoning was that such a law would create informers, and the appearance of informers is the worst thing that can happen to a democratic society, an affront to human dignity and the right to privacy. The French Assembly refused to allow its citizens to be subjected to casual suspicion.

In China, if I suspect that you harbor bad intentions, I'll just trot over and "make a report," and never think twice about it. In fact, such behavior is praised for demonstrating "a high sense of alertness," and "an elevated class consciousness." But it also runs completely counter to democracy, and it demonstrates a lack of comprehension about fundamental human rights. No one should be subjected to casual suspicion or forced to live under constant terror. But in China people have long lived in perpetual terror, afraid of someone reporting on them even when they have done nothing wrong. If I look suspicious in the least, whether I've done anything or not, you'll rush right out and report me. Democracy will never take root in such an environment. . . .

The intellectual realm must be independent and have its own values.

This is an essential guarantee of democracy. It is only when you know something independently that you are free from relying on authorities outside the intellectual domain, such as the government. Unfortunately, things are not this way in China. I have discussed this problem with educators. In the past, even during "the seventeen years" [1949 to 1966, the era prior to the Cultural Revolution], our universities were mainly engaged in producing tools, not in educating human beings. Education was not concerned with helping students to become critical thinkers, but with producing docile instruments to be used by others. Chinese intellectuals need to insist on thinking for themselves and using their own judgment, but I'm afraid that even now we have not grasped this lesson. . . .

Question: Surely we can't pin our hopes on the Communist Party's reforming itself peacefully and carrying out "complete Westernization"? In your heart of hearts, do you really think that the Party can remove the cancer that has spread all through it? Or do we, in the end, need another people's revolution?

Fang: I think I can answer this question. The Communist Party faces a great many problems. Behind closed doors, the assessment is that even if the reforms are successful, the Party will still be in serious trouble. Some people will ask how I can say such things in public, but I think that the Party is in a situation where it has to reform whether it wants to or not. If all of China awakens to this fact, starting with all the students, and all the young intellectuals, and finally all the other intellectuals, then things will change. And if there were no change, the country would get rid of the Party.

Whether the Party reforms itself or not won't be determined by some leader, but by all the forces of history. We shouldn't think that the Party can remain totally isolated from the masses; it's impossible. . . .

So when you ask if the Party is going to reform itself, you have to look at the society as a whole. Of course, if the leaders are good, that's great. But even if the leaders aren't good, as long as the masses can slowly absorb the most progressive Western cultural influences, then there will be change, one way or another. Now, as to how change is achieved: Will it definitely take violence? I think—especially after seeing both the East and the West—that there are many pathways available. As soon as we think about change, we think of political power growing from the barrel of a gun. We are conditioned by our ideology to think that any kind of change requires a gun.

But I think that in the West, many reforms have succeeded without taking such a drastic course. They have followed the path of gradual reform. Reform is not an absolute impossibility. Last year was better than the year before, this year better than last year, and maybe next year will bring still more improvement. . . . Don't underestimate the power of incremental change.

30

Government Representatives Meet with Students
April 29, 1989

Though discussions about the need for democratic reform continued on university campuses, they did not break out into the open until the death of Hu Yaobang. Hu's funeral on April 22, 1989, widely disappointed students, many of whom felt that the petition of the kneeling students ought to have been received, preferably by Premier Li Peng. Two days later, a student boycott shut down nearly all Beijing universities. A march on April 27 attracted at least a hundred thousand, including many who were not students; it appeared to be a real breakthrough into public politics. In this context of rising conflict, the government arranged a staged, and publicly broadcast, "dialogue" with student representatives. The regime participants were Yuan Mu, spokesman of the State Council (and thus a senior figure, but not involved in policy); He Dongchang, chair of the State Education Commission; and Yuan Liben of the Beijing Municipal Communist Party Committee. In this way, the government clearly hoped to defuse student discontent; the question was what students hoped to gain. Simply to be able to question a midlevel official on television was an achievement, but what exactly was the point of the dialogue?

Yuan Mu: Entrusted by the State Council and Comrade Li Peng, I and concerned comrades of the State Education Commission and Beijing Municipality have come here to hold a discussion, a dialogue, with you today.

Leading comrades of our party and state are showing great concern for the broad masses of students. They asked me to speak to you and through you to speak to the broad masses of students of schools of higher learning in the capital. They hope that the broad masses of students will return to their classes as quickly as possible. . . . The broad masses of students, filled with patriotic enthusi-

From "Yuan Mu and Others Hold Dialogue with Students," in *Beijing Spring, 1989: Confrontation and Conflict—The Basic Documents*, ed. Michael Oksenberg, Lawrence R. Sullivan, and Marc Lambert (Armonk, N.Y.: M. E. Sharpe, 1990), 218–21, 223, 225–26, 229–30, 233–35, 241–44.

asm, hope to promote democracy, strengthen the reform, punish those guilty of embezzlement, and overcome corruption. All those wishes are in complete accord with the wishes of the party and the government. . . .

We can say that at present our country is faced with many difficulties, and it would be even more difficult to overcome those difficulties if there are disturbances and instability. They hope that you students and people of all circles in the society will strive to support the party and the government, adhere to the four cardinal principles,[1] keep to the general policy of reform and opening to the outside world, carry out the reform and open policy, and promote socialist modernization through to the end and achieve our desired victories. Before I came here, the leading comrades of the party and state asked me to make these remarks to you students.

Now if you have any questions, please ask them. . . .

Student: I am Xiang Xiaoqi, a postgraduate student in the study of international law at the University of Political Science and Law. . . .

The meeting today can only be regarded as a preliminary one aimed at creating a tranquil atmosphere and smoothing out the channels for dialogue. This is not the official form of dialogue demanded by the broad masses of students. . . .

Yuan Mu: With regard to this statement, I would like to express my views. The form of dialogue can be varied, I think. Our dialogue is not a negotiation between opponents. . . . There is no negotiation existing between the government and the students. Today's form of dialogue is fine, if the students wish to express their views. . . . Dialogue means getting together and engaging in conversation, exchanging ideas, and deepening understanding. So long as we conduct dialogue in this manner without setting preconditions, today's dialogue will certainly help facilitate the exchange of views, I think. . . .

Student: I am Chang Weijun of the College of Architectural Engineering. I would like to ask Comrade Yuan a question. To lead an austere life, we need the proper atmosphere. We should share weal and woe. Some people golf every Sunday in the company of their wives. Is there not a big gap between this practice and the material life of the whole people as well as the spirit of working together to tide over difficulties? [Applause.]

---

[1] Outlined by Deng Xiaoping in 1979, the four cardinal principles called for upholding socialism, the people's democratic dictatorship, the Chinese Communist party, and Marxist-Leninist-Maoist thought.

I have with me issue No. 2 for 1989 of the magazine *Jiankang zhi-nan* [Guide to health]. On page 48 is a report on an excellent golfer. There is also a color picture here. . . .

[Another student holds up a copy of *Jiankang zhinan*, showing a page which reads: "Excellent golfer — Zhao Ziyang."[2] The page also shows four color photos of Zhao Ziyang playing golf.]

Yuan Mu: I will forward this student's opinion to the leading comrades concerned. There are still very few golfers in China. Students think it is unnecessary. Sometimes, however, for the sake of international intercourse, it is permissible to golf a little. But do not overdo it. But I do not know the actual situation and cannot tell if golf was played every Sunday. If this is true, I will convey this message to the leader. . . .

Unidentified student: I am a student of the Department of Management of the Beijing Aeronautical Engineering Institute, admitted in 1986. . . . The most important questions that need to be answered today are the questions we raised in the student strike. Therefore, our dialogue must be held with the party and state leaders. However, no party and state leaders are present here today; thus, today's dialogue cannot answer any questions raised in the student strike. So this is not the dialogue we students asked for. So I, representing myself, have decided to leave this meeting room. Fellow students who support my opinion, please also leave. . . . [Video shows student leaving alone, while other students raise their hands asking for the floor.] . . .

He Dongchang: Please let me say a few words. Regarding our students of schools of higher learning in the capital as well as students of the entire country, I, myself, and staff members of the State Education Commission, adult comrades, teachers and presidents of various schools all have the same frame of mind, that is, they want to love students as they love their dearest children. Even if the students make mistakes, we will help them correct their mistakes. In other words, if there are 160,000 students in the capital, we have such feelings toward more than 99 percent of them. However, we must guard against those who hide behind you and whom you students don't know. Those people are only a small handful, but it merits our attention to watch them. . . .

---

[2]*Zhao Ziyang* (1919–2005): general secretary of the Chinese Communist party (1987–1989). Ironically, Zhao Ziyang turned out to be a proponent of real dialogue with the students in Tiananmen Square. In his posthumous memoirs, *Prisoner of the State: The Secret Journal of Premier Zhao Ziyang* (New York: Simon & Schuster, 2009), he argues that China needs Western-style democracy.

Student: I am Fu Haifeng, a student of the 1988 class of the Department of International Politics at Beijing University. I was one of the representatives who went down on their knees in front of the Great Hall of the People on April 22. . . .

As a participant and witness of history, I would like to raise . . . questions regarding the circumstances at that time. . . . The 100,000 students sat quietly for several hours and the three representatives went down on their knees for thirty minutes, expressing our strong desire to hold a dialogue with the government. Why didn't the government send an official to talk to the students and their representatives? Instead, only two staff members of the funeral committee showed up. . . .

Yuan Liben: . . . The three students' kneeling down, to tell the truth, surprised everyone. Under such circumstances, those common public functionaries could not help but wonder what to do because they are just common public functionaries. I think you should understand this point. . . . Compared with the main demands of our students, . . . I think this was just a very small incident. We already have clearly explained the events. . . .

Yuan Liben: . . . I feel that regardless of the form of dialogue and regardless of whether or not the participants are representative of the students, dialogue is comprehensive only when it serves to help understand the thinking of people from all strata and all walks of life. . . .

For instance, today we have understood the views of many students and the problems they have. As for solutions, I agree that the purpose of dialogue is to find solutions. However, we must not be metaphysical. We must not think that all problems have solutions once dialogue is held. If we think like this, then we are guilty of holding an oversimplified view of our country's entire modernization process. Some of the questions raised by the students can be answered, especially certain specific questions raised to clarify certain facts. Some questions can be explained to the students. Some questions need to be reported and further studied. Certain questions, in particular, require a legal process. . . .

Student: I am Zhang Zhaohui from the Department of Chinese at Beijing Teachers University. Leaders have often said that we should draw a line of demarcation between troublemaking by a handful of people and the good will of the vast number of students. Now I would like to ask: What is the central authorities' assessment of the recent student movement joined by over 100,000 students in

Beijing, and how will the central authorities deal with the student organizers of the movement? . . .

He Dongchang: In giving equal stress to democracy and the legal system, we handle problems in the spirit of democracy and according to the law. So long as one does not violate the provisions of state laws and decrees, he or she is innocent. This applies to people in general, including students, teachers, and other citizens. Even before the student movement took place, I, as an official of the Education Commission, believed that young students who engaged in improper behavior or speech out of excitement should be totally forgiven. This is still my attitude [applause]. . . .

Student: I am Jiang Jingcheng, a student from the Beijing College of Leadership and Economic Management, admitted in 1987. I wish to point out that two large-scale student demonstrations were held on April 21 and 27. The demonstrators were cheered and assisted by hundreds of thousands of Beijing residents who lined the procession route. Some people carried weaker students on bicycles and trishaws, while others offered money, cigarettes, and food, shouting "Long live college students," "The people support you," and other slogans. Some people even broke into tears and were moved by the students' enthusiasm and sincerity. Doesn't this show that the students' movement should be affirmed and that it accords with popular sentiments? What is the government's explanation of these incidents?

Yuan Mu: We addressed this question at the very beginning of this meeting, as well as in many of our replies to other questions. Out of patriotic enthusiasm, most students wanted to express their desire to promote democracy, to deepen reform, to punish corrupt officials and official racketeers, and so on. This is completely understandable to the party and the government, both of which consider the students' desire to be entirely in accord with the goal that the party and government should strive to achieve in their work. . . .

Student: I am a student in the Department of Law at the University of Political Science and Law. My name is Wu Junjie. . . .

First, I would like to talk about the views put forward by the editorial of *Renmin ribao*,[3] on April 26. At present, the broad masses of fellow students are of the opinion that they cannot agree with the term "disturbance." We are not creating a disturbance. Second, my

---

[3] *Renmin ribao: People's Daily*, the official newspaper of the Communist party.

fellow students do not agree with the term "a handful of people." Most students have taken part in this activity. The editorial, the broad masses of students believe, is a calumniation and smear against the students. Third, they do not agree with the editorial's determination of the nature of the students' demonstration as an activity that advocates opposition to the party and the government. The broad masses of fellow students still love their country. . . .

Yuan Liben: . . . Students should know that the government is not opposed to them. Although we disapprove of some of your actions, from the bottom of our hearts, we still regard you as children, and you are our students. This is the basic idea. I hope students will go back and convey this idea to other students. You can also calmly analyze the two demonstrations. This much I have to say. . . .

He Dongchang: We have different views on some problems. It depends on how you look at it. I think we can take our time. We should seek truth from facts. Regarding the matters involving the University of Political Science and Law, the armed police, and Tiananmen, students may check with the armed police. I think we should seek truth from facts by conducting studies and investigations. We should not handle things based on our feelings. There is a song called "Move Ahead by Following Our Feelings." We cannot move ahead by simply following our feelings.

31

Hunger Strikers' Announcement
May 12, 1989

The decision to stage a hunger strike and to conduct it in Tiananmen Square was the pivotal moment of the protests of spring 1989. A hunger strike is a ritual; some hunger strikers proclaim they are fasting for a certain number of days, while others vow to fast until death. The latter form,

"Hunger Strike Announcement," in *Beijing Spring, 1989: Confrontation and Conflict — The Basic Documents*, ed. Michael Oksenberg, Lawrence R. Sullivan, and Marc Lambert (Armonk, N.Y.: M. E. Sharpe, 1990), 258–60.

which these student protesters adopted, is analogous to a self-immolation, as the strikers aim to inspire or shake up their fellow citizens while shaming the authorities through sacrifice. It is an ambiguous weapon, though, because even if the demands include dialogue or compromise, the radical form of the protest seems to preclude such responses. This hunger strike lasted a week; another one, launched by four prominent cultural-intellectual figures, began two days before the June 4 crackdown.

In this bright sunny month of May, we are on a hunger strike. In this best moment of our youth, we have no choice but to leave behind us everything beautiful about life. But how reluctant, how unwilling we are!

However, the country has come to this juncture: rampant inflation; widespread illegal business dealings by corrupt officials; the dominance of abusive power; the corruption of bureaucrats; the fleeing of a large number of good people to other countries; and the deterioration of law and order. Compatriots and all fellow countrymen with a conscience, at this critical moment of life and death of our people, please listen to our voice:

This country is our country,

The people are our people.

The government is our government.

Who will shout if we don't?

Who will act if we don't?

Although our shoulders are still tender, although death for us is still seemingly too harsh to bear, we have to part with life. When history demands us to do so, we have no choice but to die.

Our national sentiment at its purest and our loyalty at its best are labeled as "chaotic disturbance"; as "with an ulterior motive"; and as "manipulated by a small gang."

We request all honorable Chinese, every worker, peasant, soldier, ordinary citizen, intellectual, and renowned individuals, government officials, police and those who fabricated our crimes to put their hands over their hearts and examine their conscience: what crime have we committed? Are we creating chaotic disturbances? We walk out of classrooms, we march, we hunger strike, we hide. Yet our feelings are betrayed time after time. We bear the suffering of hunger to pursue the truth, and all we get is the beatings of the police. When we kneel down to beg for democracy, we are being ignored. Our request for dialogue on equal terms is met with delay after delay. Our student leaders encounter personal dangers.

What do we do?

Democracy is the most noble meaning of life; freedom is a basic human right. But the price of democracy and freedom is our life. Can the Chinese people be proud of this?

We have no other alternative but to hunger strike. We have to strike. It is with the spirit of death that we fight for life.

But we are still children, we are still children! Mother China, please take a hard look at your children. Hunger is ruthlessly destroying their youth. Are you really not touched when death is approaching them?

We do not want to die. In fact, we wish to continue to live comfortably because we are in the prime years of our lives. We do not wish to die; we want to be able to study properly. Our homeland is so poor. It seems irresponsible of us to desert our homeland to die. Death is definitely not our pursuit. But if the death of a single person or a number of persons would enable a larger number of people to live better, or if the death can make our homeland stronger and more prosperous, then we have no right to drag on an ignoble existence.

When we are suffering from hunger, moms and dads, please don't be sad. When we bid farewell to life, uncles and aunts, please don't be heart-broken. Our only hope is that the Chinese people will live better. We have only one request: please don't forget that we are definitely not after death. Democracy is not the private matter of a few individuals, and the enterprise of building democracy is definitely not to be accomplished in a single generation.

It is through death that we await a far-reaching and perpetual echo by others.

When a person is about to die, he speaks from his heart. When a horse is about to die, its cries are sad.

Farewell comrades, take care, the same loyalty and faith bind the living and the dead.

Farewell loved ones, take care. I don't want to leave you, but I have to part with life.

Farewell moms and dads, please forgive us. Your children cannot have loyalty to our country and filial piety to you at the same time.

Farewell fellow countrymen, please permit us to repay our country in the only way left to us. The pledge that is delivered by death will one day clear the sky of our republic.

The reasons of our hunger strike are: first, to protest the cold and apathetic attitude of our government towards the students' strike; second, to protest the delay of our higher learning; and third, to protest the government's continuous distortions in its reporting of this patriotic and democratic movement of students, and their labeling it as a "chaotic disturbance."

The demands from the hunger strikers are: first, on equal basis, the government should immediately conduct concrete and substantial dialogues with the delegation of Beijing institutes of higher learning. Second, the government should give this movement a correct name, a fair and unbiased assessment, and should affirm that this is a patriotic and democratic students' movement.

The date for the hunger strike is 2:00 p.m., May 13; location, Tiananmen Square.

This is not a chaotic disturbance. Its name should be immediately rectified. Immediate dialogue! No more delays! Hunger strike for the people! We have no choice. We appeal to world opinion to support us. We appeal to all democratic forces to support us.

32

CHAI LING

I Am Still Alive

June 8, 1989

Chai Ling, then just twenty-three years old, became one of the most prominent participants in the Tiananmen protests at about the time of the hunger strike. She was the leader of the Hunger Strike Council, which essentially ran the occupation of Tiananmen Square. During the three weeks that students occupied the square, it became the center of the attention of the world's media. Workers, students, and other groups staged marches that culminated there; artists built a nine-meter Goddess of Democracy statue. Late in the evening of June 3, a "Democracy University" began meeting.

But the regime had declared martial law on May 19 and was moving inexorably toward confrontation. So too were the students, and Chai

From Chai Ling, "I Am Still Alive," in *Voices from Tiananmen Square: Beijing Spring and the Democracy Movement*, ed. Mok Chiu Yu and J. Frank Harrison (Montreal: Black Rose Books, 1990), 194–200.

Ling was among those pushing a more forceful line. One factor in the regime's decision to send in the army was the lack of any possible external pressure; another was that the economy had not sapped the strength of the ruling elite (as it still has not today). But the ritualized nature of opposition, and perhaps the very vagueness of the protesters' goals, may also have made any other outcome, such as democratic transformation, unlikely. It is important, in reading this document, to remember that it was composed a few days after the crackdown, from the relative safety of Hong Kong. The author is recalling the events but also, presumably, reshaping them as we all do with our memories.

Today is June 8th, 1989. It is now 4:00 p.m. I am Chai Ling, Commander-in-Chief in Tiananmen Square. I am still alive.

I believe I am the best qualified witness to the situation in the Square during the period from June 2nd to 4th June, and I also have the responsibility to tell that truth to everyone, every single countryman, every single citizen. . . .

Now, let me briefly describe our position. I was Commander-in-Chief in the Square, where at that time there was a broadcasting station for the hunger strike group. I stayed there throughout, directing the activities of all the students in the Square. . . . We received constant and urgent messages, from every direction, that students and citizens were being beaten and harassed. . . .

Around 7:00 or 8:00 p.m. we, the commanding unit, had held a press conference, and told both local and foreign reporters as much as we knew of the situation . . . The commanding unit made one statement, saying that the only slogan we held was, "Down with Li Peng's false Government."

At 9:00 p.m. sharp, all of the students in the Square stood up and with their right hands raised, declared: "I vow that, for the promotion of our nation's process of democratization, for the true prosperity of our nation, for our great nation, for defense against a handful of schemers for the salvation of our 1.1 billion countrymen from White Terror,[1] that I will give up my young life to protect Tiananmen Square,

---

[1]The term *white terror* dates back to the French Revolution, when it referred to massacres carried out by supporters of the monarchy. Ever since, participants in many revolutions have used the term to label powerful opponents (in this case, the Chinese Communist regime) as antirevolutionary.

to protect the Republic. Heads can fall, blood can run, but the people's Square can never be abandoned. We are willing to sacrifice our young lives in a fight to the death of the very last person."

At 10:00 p.m. sharp, the Democratic University was formally established in the Square, with vice-commander Jiang Deli becoming the principal, and people from all sides celebrated the occasion enthusiastically. At that time, the commanding unit was receiving many urgent warnings, as the situation became very tense. On one hand, there was the thunderous applause for the establishment of our Democratic University in the northern part of the Square near the Statue of the Goddess of Liberty; whereas along the Boulevard of Eternal Peace at the eastern edge of the Square, there was a river of blood. Murderers, those soldiers of the 27th Battalion, used tanks, heavy machine guns, bayonets (tear gas being already outdated) on people who did no more than utter a slogan, or throw a stone. They chased after the people, shooting with their machine guns. All the corpses along the Boulevard of Eternal Peace bled heavily from their chests; and all the students who ran to us were bleeding in the arms, chests and legs. They did this to their own countrymen, taking their life's blood. The students were very angry and held their dead friends in their arms.

After 10:00 p.m. we, the commanding unit, made a request based upon the principle that our Patriotic-Democratic Movement, as both a Student Movement and People's Movement, had always been to demonstrate peacefully. In opposition, therefore, to the many students and citizens who angrily declared that it was time to use weapons, we proposed the supreme principle of peace and sacrifice.

In this way, hands joined together, shoulder to shoulder, singing "The Internationale,"[2] we slowly came out from our tents. Hands joined, we came to the western, northern and the southern sides of the Monument of the People's Heroes,[3] and sat there quietly, with serenity in our eyes, waiting for the attack by murderers. What we were involved in was a battle between love and hate, not one between violence and military force. We all knew that if we used things like clubs, gasoline bottles and the like (which are hardly weapons) against those soldiers,

---

[2]"The Internationale," composed in France in 1871, became the best-known anthem of the Socialist movement worldwide.

[3]*Monument of the People's Heroes*: a huge obelisk on Tiananmen Square, completed in 1958 to honor Chinese revolutionaries of the nineteenth and twentieth centuries.

who were holding machine guns or riding in tanks, and who were out of their minds, then this would have been the greatest tragedy for our Democracy Movement.

So the students sat there silently, waiting to give up their lives. There were loudspeakers next to the commanding unit's tent playing "The Descendants of the Dragon."[4] We sang along with it, with tears in our eyes. We embraced each other, shook hands, because we knew that the last moment of our lives, the moment to give up our lives for our nation, had arrived.

. . . People of the Republic, you must not forget the children who fought for you.

Between 2:00 and 3:00 a.m. on June 4th, we had to abandon our headquarters at the bottom of the Monument and move to the Monument's platform to continue our command of the Square. As Commander-in-Chief, I went with my deputy, Li Lu, to visit the students around the Monument, to give them moral support. The students just sat there quietly. They told me they would sit there in the first row, steadfast and immovable. Students in the back row said they, too, would remain steadfast. "We would not be afraid even if the front row of students was beaten and killed. We would continue to sit still and not withdraw. We would not retaliate and kill."

I chatted with the students and told them the old story that goes: "There were these 1.1 billion ants living on a mountain top. One day, the mountain was ablaze. To survive, the ants had to get down the mountain. They gathered themselves into a giant ball and rolled down the mountain. The ants on the outside were burnt to death. But the lives of many more were saved. My fellow students, we at the Square are the outermost layer, because in our hearts we understand that only by dying can we ensure the survival of the Republic." The students sang the *Internationale* again and again. They held hands tightly. . . . We decided to leave.

But the executioners didn't keep their word. As students were leaving, armed troops charged up to the third level of the Monument. They didn't wait for us to inform everyone of the decision to leave. They had already shot our loudspeakers to pieces. That was the Monument to the People's Heroes. They dared to open fire at the Monument. Most of the students withdrew. With tears in our eyes, we

---

[4]*"Descendants of the Dragon"*: a song by Hou Dejian, a well-known singer who joined the students on Tiananmen Square. The term *descendants of the dragon* refers to the Chinese (Han) people.

started to leave the Square. People told us not to cry. We said we would be back, because this is the People's Square. . . .

Then the tanks made "mincemeat" of them. Some say more than 200 students died. Some say more than 4000 died in the Square alone. I don't know the total. But the members of the Independent Workers' Union were on the outside. They stood their ground and they're all dead. There were twenty to thirty of them. I heard that, after the students left, tanks and armored personnel carriers flattened tents with bodies inside. They poured gasoline over them and burned them. Then they washed away the traces with water. Our movement's symbol, the Goddess of Democracy, was crushed to bits.

With locked arms, we went around Chairman Mao's Memorial toward the south of the Square. That was when we first saw tens of thousands of helmeted soldiers. The students ran toward them and yelled: "Dogs. Fascists." So we headed west, and saw ranks upon ranks of soldiers running toward the Square. Civilians, students, though hoarse from all the yelling, continued to shout: "Fascists, dogs, beasts." But they were ignored by the soldiers, who kept on running toward "our" Square. . . .

The radio kept saying that the troops had come to Beijing to deal with riotous elements and to maintain order in the capital. I think I'm most qualified to say that we students are not riotous elements. Anyone with a conscience should put his hand on his chest and think of children, arm in arm, shoulder to shoulder, sitting quietly under the Monument, their eyes awaiting the executioner's blade. Can they be riotous elements? If they were riotous elements, would they sit there quietly? . . .

We who walked away from Tiananmen Square arrived at Beijing University, still alive. Many students from other universities, students from out of town, had prepared beds to welcome us. But we were very, very sad. We were alive. Many more were left in the Square, and on Changan Avenue. They'll never come back. Some of them were very young. They will never come back.

As we entered Beijing University, our hunger strike turned sit-in, our peaceful protest, came to an end. . . .

But my compatriots, even at the darkest moment, dawn will still break. Even with the frenzied, fascist crackdown, a true people's democratic republic will be born. The critical moment has come. My compatriots, all Chinese nationals with a conscience, all Chinese people, wake up! The ultimate victory must be the people's! Yang Shangkun, Li Peng, Wang Zhen and Bo Yibo,[5] the final hour of your puppet regime is near!

Down with Fascism!
Down with Military Rule!
Long Live the Republic!

[5]*Yang Shangkun* (1907–1998), *Li Peng* (1928–), *Wang Zhen* (1908–1993), *and Bo Yibo* (1908–2007): president, premier, vice president, and a senior member of the Communist party leadership, respectively.

A Chronology of Democratic Revolutions
(1968–1995)

1968   Student rebellions in most countries of Western Europe and the United States; Prague Spring reform movement in Czechoslovakia; height of Cultural Revolution in China.

1973   *September* General Augusto Pinochet overthrows Salvador Allende, president of Chile.

1974   *April* "Carnation Revolution" in Portugal, seen by some as the first nonviolent, democratic political transformation.

1975   Helsinki Accords are signed, affirming governments' protection of human rights.

1976   *June* Soweto Uprising in South Africa.

1977   Human rights groups emerge in Eastern Europe and the Soviet Union.

1978   *October* Cardinal Karol Wojtyła of Poland is elected pope.

        December Democracy Wall movement begins in China, as does Deng Xiaoping's Four Modernizations campaign.

1979   *February* Iranian Revolution brings Ayatollah Khomeini to power.

        December Soviet Union invades Afghanistan.

1980   *March* Archbishop Óscar Romero assassinated in San Salvador, El Salvador.

        April Zimbabwe, the former British colony of Southern Rhodesia, gains independence.

        August After several weeks of strikes, Polish authorities agree to the formation of Solidarity.

1981   *December* General Wojciech Jaruzelski declares martial law in Poland, ultimately outlawing Solidarity.

1983   *May* Massive strikes in Chile signal the return of popular public protest.

August Benigno Aquino returns to the Philippines and is assassinated.

August United Democratic Front is formed in South Africa.

October Argentina holds democratic elections, bringing an end to dictatorship.

November White South African voters approve a new constitution extending limited franchise to "coloreds" and Indians, but not to blacks.

1985 *March* Mikhail Gorbachev becomes general secretary of the Communist party of the Soviet Union.

August National Accord for Transition to Full Democracy is signed in Chile.

November Gorbachev and U.S. president Ronald Reagan meet in Geneva.

December Congress of South African Trade Unions (COSATU) forms; COSATU, the African National Congress (ANC), and the United Democratic Front (UDF) begin a campaign of resistance.

1986 *February* Protests force Haitian dictator Jean-Claude "Baby Doc" Duvalier to step down.

February Ferdinand Marcos is defeated by Corazon Aquino in the race for president and flees the Philippines.

April Explosion and fire destroy the nuclear power plant at Chernobyl, Ukraine, USSR.

September Chilean Communists make failed attempt on Augusto Pinochet's life.

December Student protests in Shanghai and other Chinese cities.

1987 *February* Voters in the Philippines approve a new constitution.

June Protests in South Korea lead to the fall of dictator Chun Doo-Hwan; democratic elections take place in December.

December First *intifada* begins among Palestinians protesting Israeli rule.

1988 *May* Soviet troops begin withdrawal from Afghanistan.

August Failed popular uprising against military dictatorship in Burma (Myanmar).

October Plebiscite vote rejects Pinochet's continued presidency in Chile.

1989 *February* Round Table discussions begin in Poland.

February F. W. de Klerk is elected National Party leader and in September becomes president of South Africa.

March Soviet Union holds elections to the Congress of People's Deputies.

April Death of reformist leader Hu Yaobang provokes student demonstrations in Beijing.

May Students in Beijing launch a hunger strike and occupy Tiananmen Square.

June Elections in Poland yield an overwhelming victory for Solidarity candidates.

June Chinese leadership initiates a crackdown against the students in Tiananmen Square.

August Hundreds of thousands of Estonians, Latvians, and Lithuanians form a human chain across the Baltic Republics, signaling their desire for independence from the Soviet Union.

November Under pressure from Gorbachev to address growing social ferment, East German Communists abruptly decide to open the Berlin Wall; "Velvet Revolution" begins in Czechoslovakia.

December Václav Havel is elected president of Czechoslovakia (by parliamentary vote).

December Free presidential election ends Pinochet's rule in Chile.

1990 *February* F. W. de Klerk legalizes the ANC and releases Nelson Mandela from prison.

March Some republics in the Soviet Union declare independence.

April President Patricio Aylwin establishes a National Truth and Reconciliation Commission to investigate crimes of the Pinochet regime.

July Ukrainian parliament declares Ukrainian sovereignty.

1991 *August* Hard-liners in the Communist hierarchy attempt a coup against Mikhail Gorbachev; Ukraine and other republics declare independence, and the Soviet Union dissolves in December.

1994 *April* South Africa's first free elections; Nelson Mandela is elected president.

1995 *July* Truth and Reconciliation Commission is created in South Africa.

Questions for Consideration

1. How would you balance long-term or underlying (structural) factors versus human factors as causes of any one of the revolutions examined in this book?
2. Participants in some revolutions employ satirical or humorous techniques, while other revolutions seem to be much graver in tone. How might these different approaches affect the course or outcome of political change? What evidence in this book supports your conclusion?
3. Compare the use of national symbols or nationalist language in the documents of two revolutions. What factors might account for the different terms used?
4. Many of the authors draw explicitly on philosophy, religion, or ideology to explain or justify their positions. Do you see evidence that different ethical or political traditions contribute to different conclusions, or are their ideas common to humanity?
5. Many of the documents call for compromise of some kind with the ruling dictatorships. What kinds of arguments do the authors use to persuade others on their side of the need for compromise?
6. What role do outside influences play, as seen by revolution participants? Identify cases in which foreign influence is seen as benign, and those in which it seems to be threatening. How do speakers and writers use this information to persuade their listeners or readers?
7. Is the concept of nonviolence a moral absolute for the authors of the documents here, or is it a tactical ploy? Can you find evidence for either position?
8. Some of the revolutions discussed here took place quite rapidly; others built up over a number of years. What effect might the rate of change have on attitudes toward violence, toward compromise, or toward the regime in general?
9. Using the Selected Bibliography, explore one of the cases in greater depth and compare it to another revolution from an earlier era, such as the Russian Revolution of 1917, the Iranian Revolution of 1979, or

the student rebellions of 1968. What similarities and differences do you find?

10. Democratic revolutions did not cease with the cold war's end. For example, Serbia in 2000, Ukraine in 2004, Lebanon in 2005, Burma in 2007, and Iran in 2009 have all experienced pro-democracy upheavals with varying degrees of success for the activists. The Internet is a rich source of journalists' and participants' accounts of these events. In what ways are these uprisings similar to the revolutions of the late cold war? How are they different?

Selected Bibliography

GENERAL

Ackerman, Peter, and Jack DuVall. *A Force More Powerful: A Century of Nonviolent Conflict.* New York: St. Martin's Press, 2000.

Brooker, Paul. *Non-democratic Regimes: Theory, Government, and Politics.* New York: Routledge, 2000.

Esposito, John L., and John O. Voll. *Islam and Democracy.* New York: Oxford University Press, 1996.

Goldstone, Jack A., Ted Robert Gurr, and Farrokh Moshiri, eds. *Revolutions of the Late Twentieth Century.* Boulder, Colo.: Westview, 1991.

Huntington, Samuel P. *The Third Wave: Democratization in the Late Twentieth Century.* Norman: University of Oklahoma Press, 1991.

Reynolds, David. *One World Indivisible: A Global History since 1945.* New York: W. W. Norton, 2000.

Schaeffer, Robert K. *Power to the People: Democratization around the World.* Boulder, Colo.: Westview Press, 1997.

Schock, Kurt. *Unarmed Insurrections: People Power Movements in Non-democracies.* Minneapolis: University of Minnesota Press, 2005.

Simpson, John. *Despatches from the Barricades: An Eye-Witness Account of the Revolutions That Shook the World, 1989–90.* London: Hutchinson, 1990.

Thompson, Mark R. *Democratic Revolutions: Asia and Eastern Europe.* London: Routledge, 2004.

Tilly, Charles. *Democracy.* Cambridge: Cambridge University Press, 2007.

Zakaria, Fareed. *The Future of Freedom: Illiberal Democracy at Home and Abroad.* New York: W. W. Norton, 2003.

Zunes, Stephen, Lester R. Kurtz, and Sarah Beth Asher. *Nonviolent Social Movements: A Geographical Perspective.* Oxford: Blackwell, 1999.

POLAND

Bernhard, Michael H. *The Origins of Democratization in Poland: Workers, Intellectuals, and Oppositional Politics, 1976–1980.* New York: Columbia University Press, 1993.

Castle, Marjorie. *Triggering Communism's Collapse: Perceptions and Power in Poland's Transition*. Lanham, Md.: Rowman and Littlefield, 2003.

Ekiert, Grzegorz. *The State against Society: Political Crises and Their Aftermath in East Central Europe*. Princeton, N.J.: Princeton University Press, 1996.

Falk, Barbara J. *The Dilemmas of Dissidence in East-Central Europe: Citizen Intellectuals and Philosopher Kings*. Budapest: Central European University Press, 2003.

Garton Ash, Timothy. *The Polish Revolution: Solidarity*. 3rd ed. New Haven, Conn.: Yale University Press, 2002.

Kenney, Padraic. *A Carnival of Revolution: Central Europe, 1989*. Princeton, N.J.: Princeton University Press, 2002.

Kubik, Jan. *The Power of Symbols against the Symbols of Power: The Rise of Solidarity and the Fall of State Socialism in Poland*. University Park: Pennsylvania State University Press, 1994.

Ost, David. *Solidarity and the Politics of Anti-politics: Opposition and Reform in Poland since 1968*. Philadelphia: Temple University Press, 1990.

Paczkowski, Andrzej. *The Spring Will Be Ours: Poland and the Poles from Occupation to Freedom*. Translated by Jane Cave. University Park: Pennsylvania State University Press, 2003.

THE PHILIPPINES

Boudreau, Vincent. *Resisting Dictatorship: Repression and Protest in Southeast Asia*. Cambridge: Cambridge University Press, 2004.

Byington, Kaa. *Bantay ng Bayan: Stories from the NAMFREL Crusade, 1984–1986*. Manila: Bookmark, 1988.

Fenton, James. *All the Wrong Places: Adrift in the Politics of the Pacific Rim*. New York: Atlantic Monthly Press, 1988.

Karnow, Stanley. *In Our Image: America's Empire in the Philippines*. New York: Random House, 1989.

Kerkvliet, Benedict J., and Resil Mojares, eds. *From Marcos to Aquino: Local Perspectives on Political Transition in the Philippines*. Honolulu: University of Hawaii Press, 1991.

Kessler, Richard J. *Rebellion and Repression in the Philippines*. New Haven, Conn.: Yale University Press, 1989.

Mercado, Paul Sagmayao, and Francisco S. Tatad. *People Power: The Philippine Revolution of 1986: An Eyewitness History*. Manila: James B. Reuter, S.J., Foundation, 1986.

Reid, Robert H., and Eileen Guerrero. *Corazon Aquino and the Brushfire Revolution*. Baton Rouge: Louisiana State University Press, 1995.

Thompson, Mark R. *The Anti-Marcos Struggle: Personalistic Rule and Democratic Transition in the Philippines*. New Haven, Conn.: Yale University Press, 1995.

CHILE

Aman, Kenneth, and Cristián Parker, eds. *Popular Culture in Chile: Resistance and Survival*. Boulder, Colo.: Westview Press, 1991.

Baldez, Lisa. *Why Women Protest: Women's Movements in Chile*. Cambridge: Cambridge University Press, 2002.

Barahona de Brito, Alexandra. *Human Rights and Democratization in Latin America: Uruguay and Chile*. Oxford: Oxford University Press, 1997.

Constable, Pamela, and Arturo Valenzuela. *A Nation of Enemies: Chile under Pinochet*. New York: W. W. Norton, 1991.

Drake, Paul W., and Iván Jaksić, eds. *The Struggle for Democracy in Chile, 1982–1990*. Lincoln: University of Nebraska Press, 1991.

Kaplan, Temma. *Taking Back the Streets: Women, Youth, and Direct Democracy*. Berkeley: University of California Press, 2003.

Oxhorn, Philip. *Organizing Civil Society: The Popular Sectors and the Struggle for Democracy in Chile*. University Park: Pennsylvania State University Press, 1995.

Puryear, Jeffrey M. *Thinking Politics: Intellectuals and Democracy in Chile, 1973–1988*. Baltimore: Johns Hopkins University Press, 1994.

Stern, Steve J. *Battling for Hearts and Minds: Memory Struggles in Pinochet's Chile, 1973–1988*. Durham, N.C.: Duke University Press, 2006.

SOUTH AFRICA

Eades, Lindsay Michie. *The End of Apartheid in South Africa*. Westport, Conn.: Greenwood Press, 1999.

Houston, Gregory F. *The National Liberation Struggle in South Africa: A Case Study of the United Democratic Front, 1983–1987*. Aldershot, U.K.: Ashgate, 1999.

Johns, Sheridan, and R. Hunt Davis Jr., eds. *Mandela, Tambo, and the African National Congress: The Struggle against Apartheid, 1948–1990*. Oxford: Oxford University Press, 1991.

Lodge, Tom, Bill Nasson, Steven Mufson, Hkehla Shubane, and Nokwanda Sithole. *All, Here, and Now: Black Politics in South Africa in the 1980s*. New York: Ford Foundation, 1991.

Marx, Anthony W. *Lessons of Struggle: South African Internal Opposition, 1960–1990*. New York: Oxford University Press, 1992.

Seekings, Jeremy. *The UDF: A History of the United Democratic Front in South Africa, 1983–1991*. Athens: Ohio University Press, 2000.

Tutu, Desmond. *Crying in the Wilderness: The Struggle for Justice in South Africa*. 2nd ed. Edited by John Webster. Grand Rapids, Mich.: Eerdmans, 1990.

Waldmeir, Patti. *Anatomy of a Miracle: The End of Apartheid and the Birth of a New South Africa*. New York: W. W. Norton, 1997.

UKRAINE

Bahry, Romana M. "Rock Culture and Rock Music in Ukraine." In *Rocking the State: Rock Music and Politics in Eastern Europe and Russia*, edited by Sabrina Petra Ramet, 243–96. Boulder, Colo.: Westview, 1994.

Batalden, Stephen K., ed. *Seeking God: The Recovery of Religious Identity in Orthodox Russia, Ukraine, and Georgia*. DeKalb: Northern Illinois University Press, 1993.

Dawson, Jane I. *Eco-nationalism: Anti-Nuclear Activism and National Identity in Russia, Lithuania, and Ukraine*. Durham, N.C.: Duke University Press, 1996.

Kuzio, Taras, and Andrew Wilson. *Ukraine: Perestroika to Independence*. New York: St. Martin's Press, 1994.

Marples, David. *The Social Impact of the Chernobyl Disaster*. New York: St. Martin's Press, 1988.

Marples, David. *Ukraine under Perestroika: Ecology, Economics, and the Workers' Revolt*. New York: St. Martin's Press, 1991.

Nahaylo, Bohdan. *The Ukrainian Resurgence: Ukraine's Road to Independence*. Toronto: University of Toronto Press, 1998.

Solchanyk, Roman. *Ukraine: From Chernobyl to Sovereignty—A Collection of Interviews*. New York: St. Martin's Press, 1992.

Wilson, Andrew. *Ukraine's Orange Revolution*. New Haven, Conn.: Yale University Press, 2005.

CHINA

Calhoun, Craig. *Neither Gods nor Emperors: Students and the Struggle for Democracy in China*. Berkeley: University of California Press, 1994.

Feigon, Lee. *China Rising: The Meaning of Tiananmen*. Chicago: Ivan R. Dee, 1990.

Han Minzhu, ed. *Cries for Democracy: Writings and Speeches from the 1989 Chinese Democracy Movement*. Princeton, N.J.: Princeton University Press, 1990.

Link, Perry. *Evening Chats in Beijing*. New York: W. W. Norton, 1994.

Mann, James. *The China Fantasy: Why Capitalism Will Not Bring Democracy to China*. New York: Penguin, 2008.

Ogden, Suzanne, Kathleen Hartford, Lawrence Sullivan, and David Zweig, eds. *China's Search for Democracy: The Student and the Mass Movement of 1989*. Armonk, N.Y.: M. E. Sharpe, 1992.

Saich, Tony, ed. *The Chinese People's Movement: Perspectives on Spring 1989*. Armonk, N.Y.: M. E. Sharpe, 1990.

Schell, Orville. *Mandate of Heaven: The Legacy of Tiananmen Square and the Next Generation of China's Leaders*. New York: Simon and Schuster, 1995.

Zhao, Dingxin. *The Power of Tiananmen: State-Society Relations and the 1989 Beijing Student Movement*. Chicago: University of Chicago Press, 2001.

Acknowledgments (continued from p. ii)

Document 1: Translated by Paul Wilson. Reprinted by permission of the translator.

Document 2: "Appendix I," from *The Courage to Stand Alone* by Wei Jingsheng, translated by Kristina M. Torgeson, copyright © 1997 by Wei Jingsheng. Used by permission of Viking Penguin, a division of Penguin Group (USA) Inc.

Document 3: Desmond Tutu, "Change or Illusion," speech given in March 1980. Courtesy of the Office of Archbishop Emeritus Desmond Tutu.

Document 4: Mehdi Bazargan, "Religion and Liberty," in Charles Kurzman, ed., *Liberal Islam: A Sourcebook* (New York: Oxford University Press, 1998), 81–84. Used by permission of Oxford University Press, Inc.

Document 6: "In Quest of Democracy," from *Freedom from Fear and Other Writings*, Revised ed. by Aung San Suu Kyi, Foreword by Václav Havel, translated by Michael Aris, copyright © 1991, 1995 by Aung San Suu Kyi and Michael Aris. Used by permission of Viking Penguin, a division of Penguin Group (USA) Inc.

Document 8: Courtesy of Solidarnosc. www.solidarnosc.org.pl/archiwum/ikzd/dokumenty/index.htm. English version available in Stan Persky and Henry Flam, eds. *The Solidarity Sourcebook.* Vancouver: New Star Books, 1982.

Document 9: From Adam Michnik, *Letters from Prison and Other Essays.* The University of California Press, 1986. Reprinted by permission of the publisher.

Document 10: Courtesy of Waldemar "Major" Fydrych and the Orange Alternative Foundation, www.pomaranczowa-alternatyna.org.

Document 13: Professor Aurora J. de Dios of Conspectus Foundation.

Document 15: Professor Aurora J. de Dios of Conspectus Foundation.

Document 17: Permission granted by Hernán Vidal, Professor, Representative, to use the play "El Concurso."

Document 18: Permission granted by Hernán Vidal, Professor, TSIL Representative, for use of article "Protest at El Mercurio" and Litany.

Document 25: Courtesy of the Ukrainian Press Agency.

Document 26: Courtesy of the Ukrainian Press Agency.

Document 29: From *Bringing Down the Great Wall* by Fang Lizhi, translated by J. Williams, copyright © 1991 by Fang Lizhi. Used by permission of Alfred A. Knopf, a division of Random House, Inc.

Document 30: Published in Federal Broadcast Information Systems and in *Beijing Spring, 1989: Confrontation and Conflict: The Basic Documents,* ed. Michel Oksenberg, Lawrence R. Sullivan, and Marc Lambert (Armonk, N.Y.: M. E. Sharpe, 1990), pp. 218–21, 225–26, 229–30, 232–35, 241–44.

Document 31: From *Beijing Spring, 1989: Confrontation and Conflict: The Basic Documents,* ed. Michel Oksenberg, Lawrence R. Sullivan, and Marc Lambert (Armonk, N.Y.: M. E. Sharpe, 1990), pp. 258–60. Translation copyright © 1990 by M. E. Sharpe, Inc. Reprinted with permission.

Document 32: Reprinted by the kind permission of Black Rose Books, Montreal, from *Voices of Tiananmen Square,* edited by Mok Chiu Yu and J. Frank Harrison, 1990, www.blackrosebooks.net.

Index

Ukraine
"Atomic Evil Out of Ukraine!" (Ukrainian
Helsinki Union), 147–49
brief history of Soviet control, 140–41
Chernobyl explosion in, 66n, 69, 141,
147–49, 154, 179
declaration of sovereignty, 141, 153, 180
democratic change in, 142
"Founding Meeting of the Native
Language Association," 150–53
Helsinki Accords and, 141
independence of, 17, 142, 180
nationalism in, 141–42, 145–46
native language of, 141, 144, 145, 146, 147,
150–53
"Open Letter to Mikhail Gorbachev"
(Chornovil), 143–46
"The Political Situation in the Ukraine and
Rukh's Task" (Drach), 153–56
restraints on independent thinking in,
143–45
strikes in, 153, 154–55
Ukrainian Greek Catholic Church, 150
Ukrainian Helsinki Union, 141, 143, 151
"Atomic Evil Out of Ukraine!" 147–49
Ukrainian Herald, 143, 145, 151
underground resistance, Michnik on, 11, 56,
61–65
United Democratic Front (UDF, South
Africa), 179
goals and tactics of, 123, 129
government banning of, 133
"Ya, the Community Is the Main Source of
Power," 129–32
United States
market liberalization policies, 17
post–cold war policies, 8, 15
presence in Chile, 8, 17, 100, 103
presence in Philippines, 8, 78, 79, 82
support of militarized dictatorships, 14,
16–17
symbolism of 9/11 in, 2
Universal Declaration of Human Rights, 6,
48–49

Uruguay, 116

Valdés, Gabriel, 15
"Speech at Democratic Alliance Rally,"
114–17
Vietnam, 4, 13
violence
in apartheid South Africa, 34, 123,
124–25, 126, 127, 129,
136–39
in Chile, 100, 101, 109–13, 115
in democratic uprisings, 9
Tiananmen Square massacre, 157,
172–77
voting freedoms, as human rights issue, 2.
See also elections

Wałęsa, Lech, 10, 11
"We Are Committed to Building a Single
Nation in Our Country" (Mandela),
136–39
Wei Jingsheng, 11, 158
brief biography of, 29
"The Fifth Modernization: Democracy,"
29–33
West Ukrainian National Republic, 140
Women for Life (Mujeres por la Vida,
Chile), 101
women's movement, in Chile, 43–46,
101, 120
World War II, 3, 55, 59, 96, 141

"Ya, the Community Is the Main Source of
Power" (United Democratic Front),
129–32
Yuan Liben, 164, 167, 169
Yuan Mu, 164–66, 168
Yugoslavia
Communist regime in, 13
socialist self-management in, 29n

Zakaria, Fareed, 15
Zhao Ziyang, 166
Zimbabwe, 34, 36n